WONDERS
of OLD

A Blank Timeline Book of World History

Created by Terri Johnson

Published by

Knowledge Quest

Gresham, Oregon

WONDERS *of* OLD

A Blank Timeline Book of World History

Created by Terri Johnson

Published by:

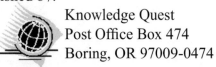

Knowledge Quest
Post Office Box 474
Boring, OR 97009-0474

www.mapsandtimelines.com

Printed in the United States of America

ISBN 1-932786-10-4 (hardback)

Cover design by Cathi Stevenson, Nova Scotia

❧ *Table of Contents* ❧

❧ *Introduction for Parents and Teachers* ❧

Dear Educator,

As you know, history is a fascinating series of interconnected events. It is amazing how seemingly unrelated happenings tie into one another. Why, for example, was the United States able to buy the Louisiana Purchase for only 2¢ an acre? Napoleon would never have sold this valuable land so cheaply unless he was desperate to fund his war efforts in western Europe. And, of course, this purchase was the catalyst for Lewis and Clark's famous exploration. We make these connections with the help of a timeline, whether it be mental or physical. As these events become congested on our timeline, we can then begin to look for the relationships between them.

This is a type of thinking we want our middle grade students to develop and our older students to fine-tune. As our children reach fifth or sixth grade (age 10-12), they begin to reason in a more logical manner. They learn to argue more effectively and think more logically. Yet this thinking needs to be carefully cultivated, not left to its own to sprout at will.

The resource of this timeline book will give your student(s) a valuable tool in making logical connections in history. Encourage him to mark significant dates/events/people from all subjects areas into his book when he encounters them in his studies. The more he records, the more connections he will make. And be careful not to draw the conclusions for him, but rather ask leading questions and allow him to have that "Ah ha!" moment of revelation that brings such satisfaction.

We, at Knowledge Quest, wish you every success in your teaching endeavors.

Blessings to you on your educational journey,

Terri Johnson

Terri Johnson

❧ *Introduction for Students* ☙

Dear young historian,

You hold in your hand a blank timeline book for you to fill in by recording the events of history. What is the point, you ask? Well, let's see...

What was significant about the year 1453AD? This was the year that Constantinople fell to the Ottoman Turks, the end of the Hundred Years' War between Britain and France, and the time of production on the Gutenberg Bible, the first printed book. These events are seemingly unrelated and yet the use of a timeline can unlock the mystery of why all of these events occurred within the same year. A timeline will give you a unique perspective of time. By seeing the events of history recorded in a linear progression, you will make connections between those events in history that you might not otherwise make as you study them separately.

A timeline will not provide you with the answers, but it will stir your curiousity and lead you to researching and discovering the answers yourself. This is what makes history fascinating.

To get the most out of this timeline tool, I would ask you to record historical events and people as you study them. Be sure to include scientists and their discoveries, inventions, famous artists and writers, virtually anything that occurred in times past. There is a list of significant events provided for you following each section of your timeline book, but this is just the tip of the iceberg. There is so much to learn and study. Don't let the list limit your entries.

If you choose to color code your entries, use this section below to choose and stay consistent with colors. By the way, gel pens or sharp colored pencils work well for writing with color. And always use your best handwriting. This may become a cherished keepsake from your school years.

Wishing you all the best,

Terri Johnson

Terri Johnson

	War/Conflict		Kings/Rulers		Laws/Ruling
	Literature		Exploration		Science
	Music		Art		Inventions
	The Bible		The Church		Medicine
	Architecture		Nations/ Empires		Religious Leaders

*"I will remember the works of the LORD: surely I will remember thy **wonders of old**. I will meditate also on all thy work, and talk of thy doings."*

...from the Old Testament, the book of Psalms, KJV, written primarily by King David of Israel c.1000BC

Timeline of Ancient History

5000BC - 400AD

Before 9000BC

9000BC

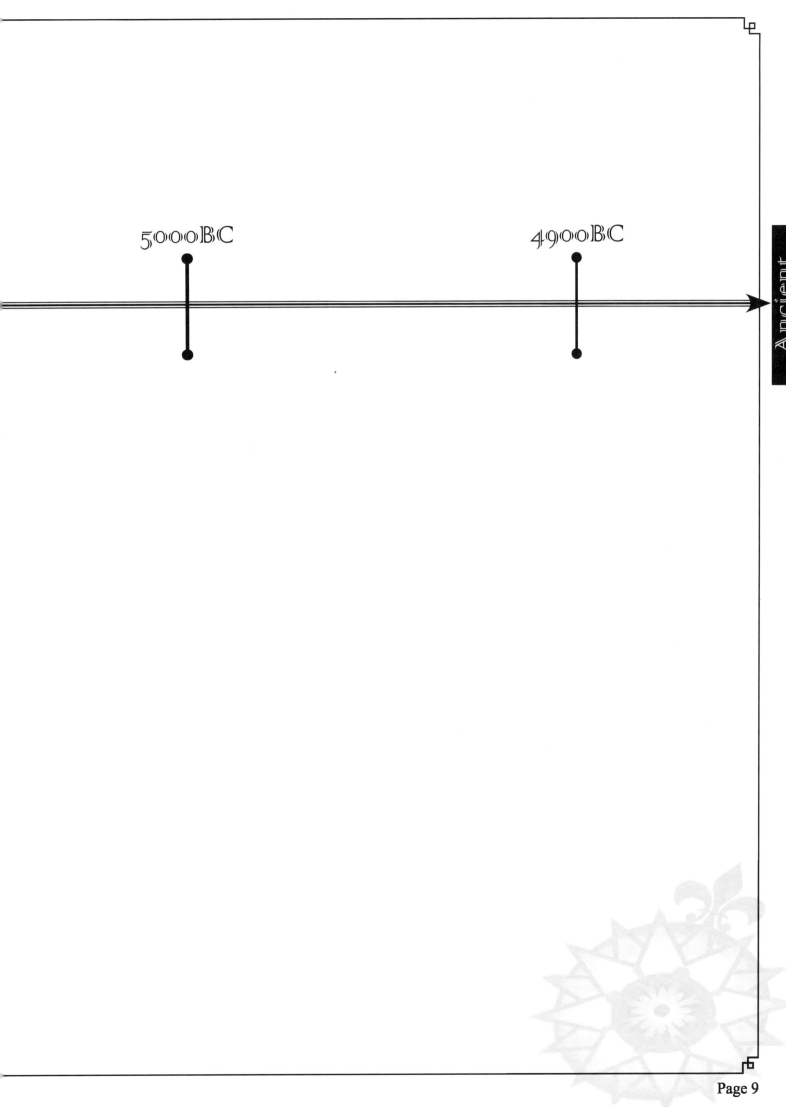

5000BC

4900BC

Ancient

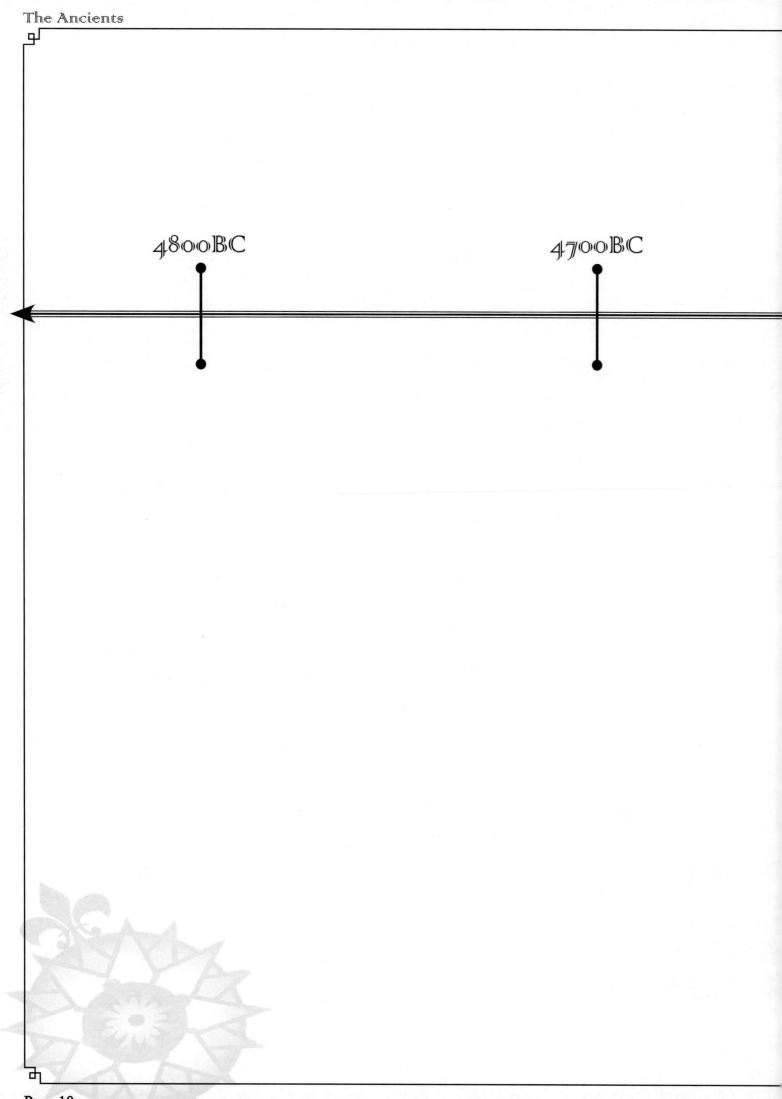

4800BC

4700BC

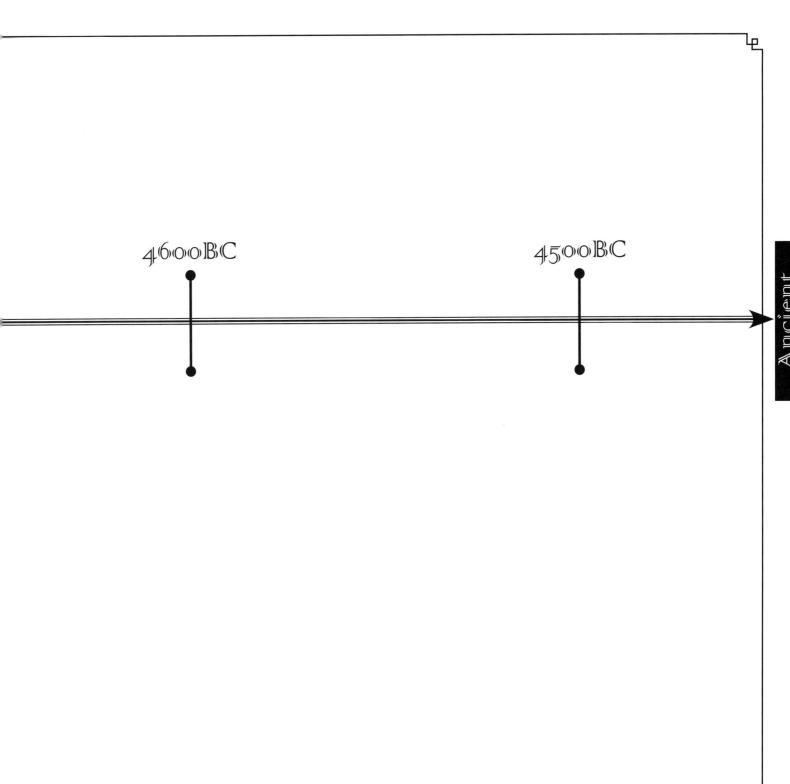

4600BC

4500BC

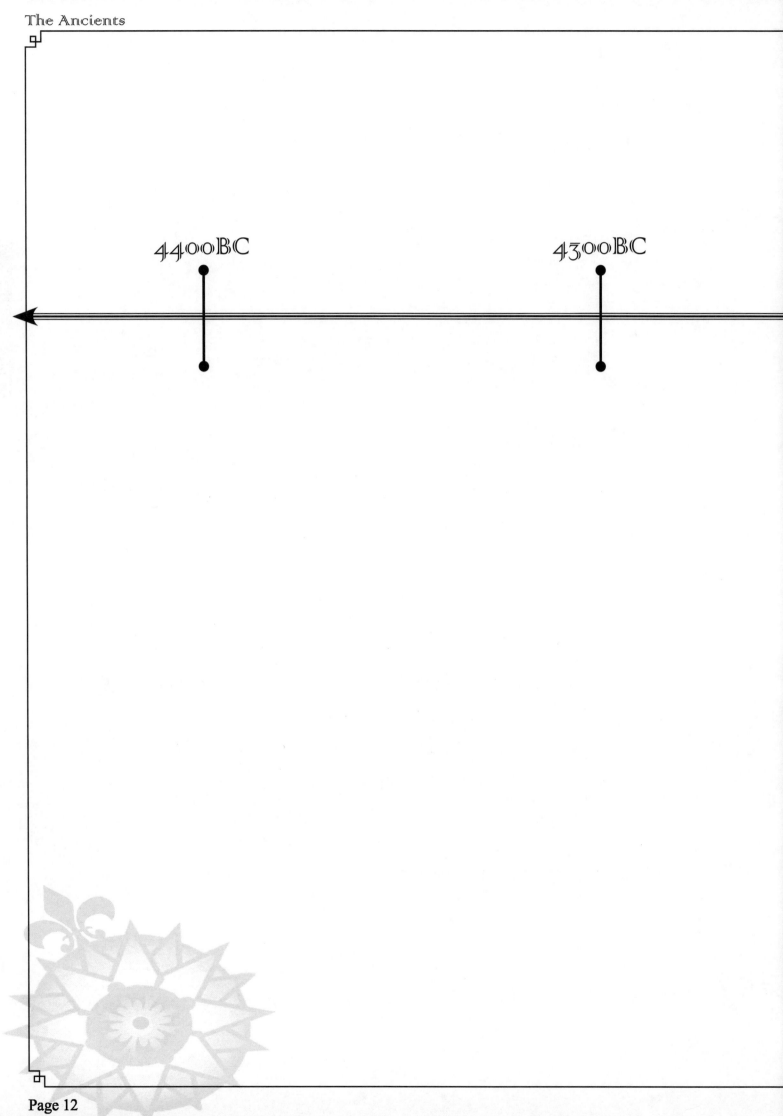

4400BC

4300BC

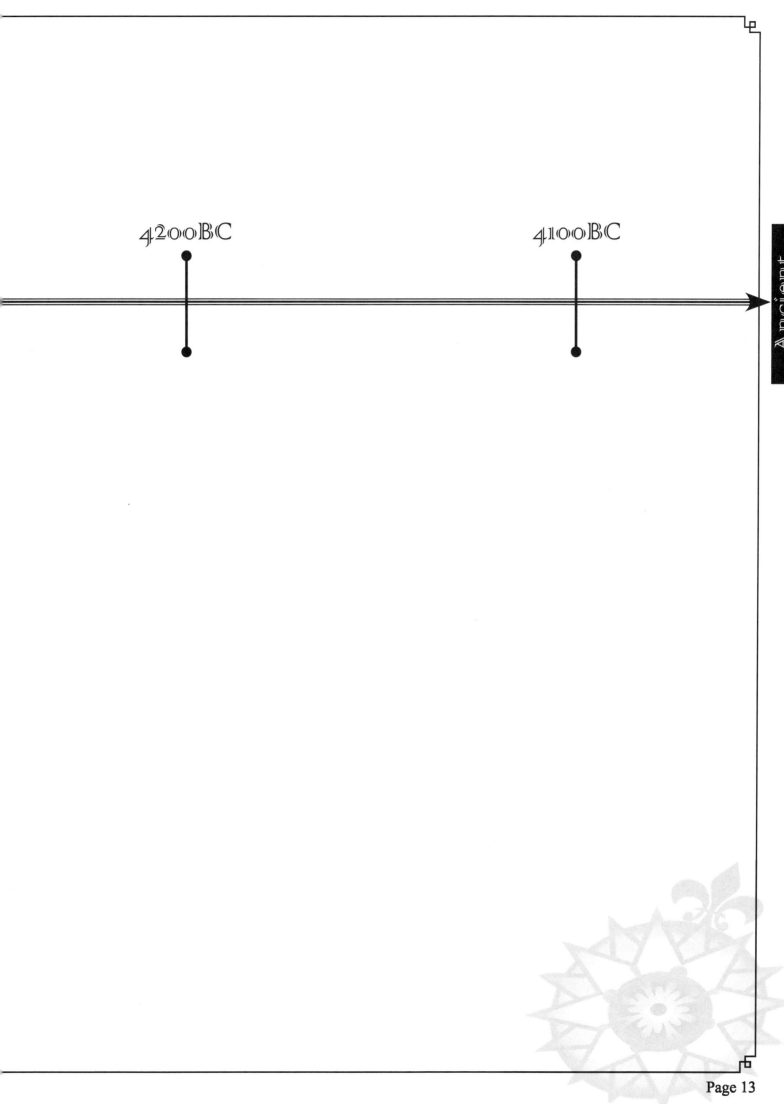

4200BC

4100BC

4000BC

3900BC

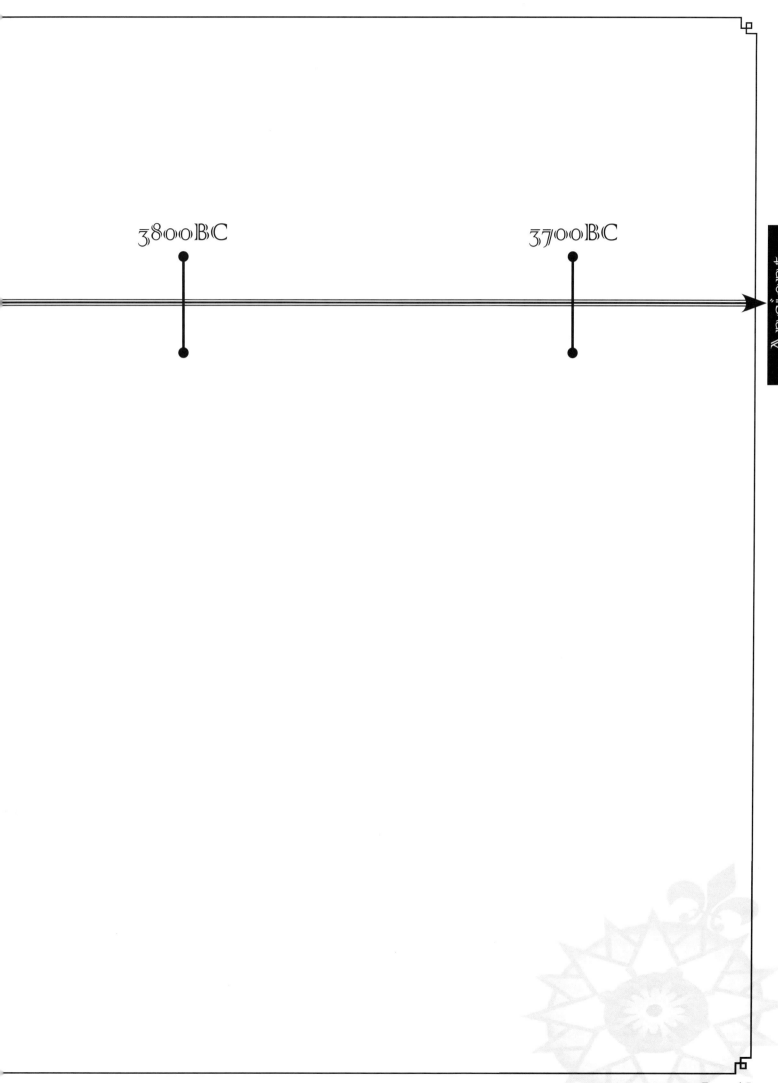

3800BC

3700BC

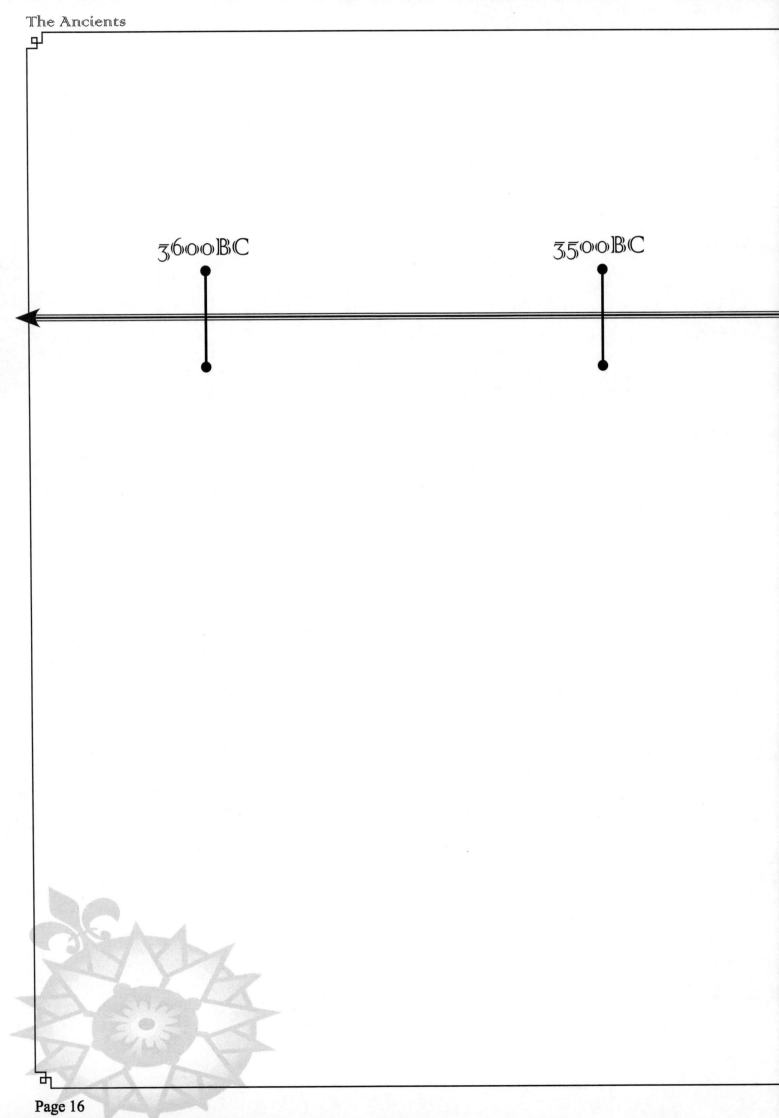

3600BC

3500BC

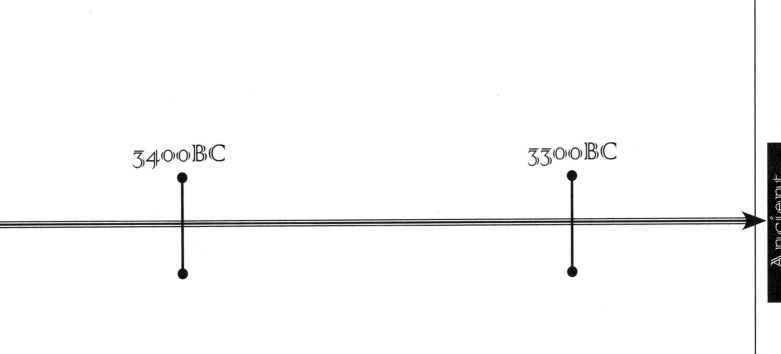

3400BC

3300BC

3200BC

3100BC

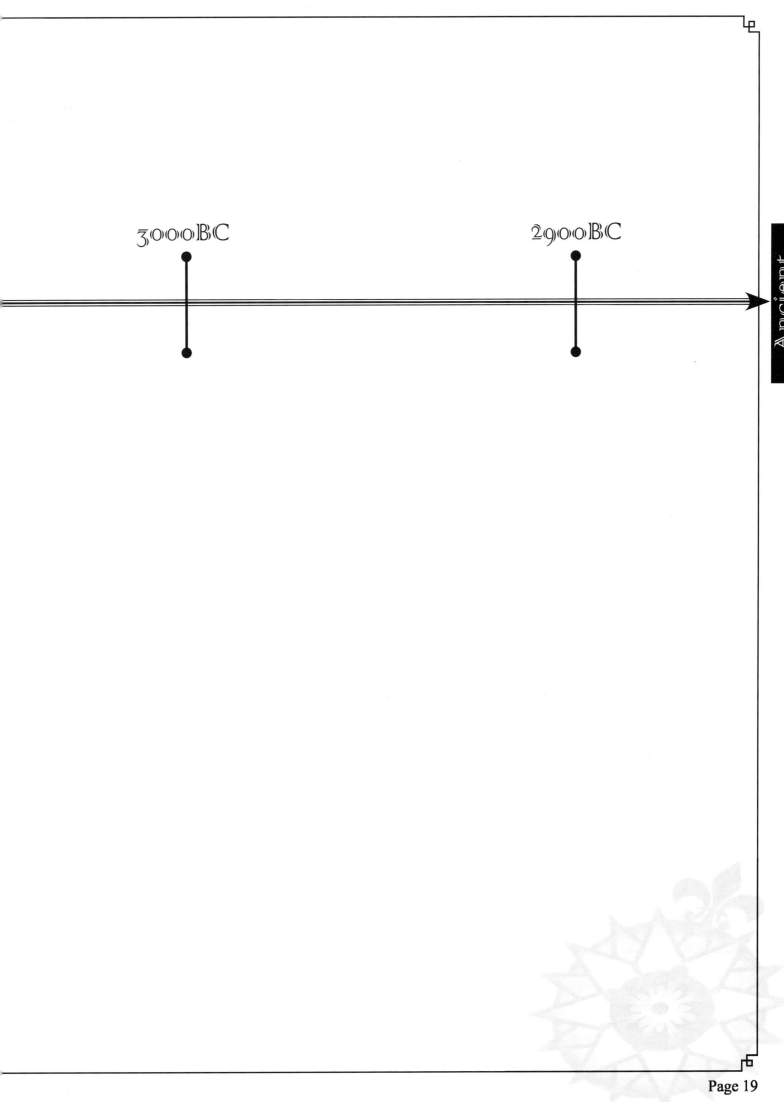

3000BC

2900BC

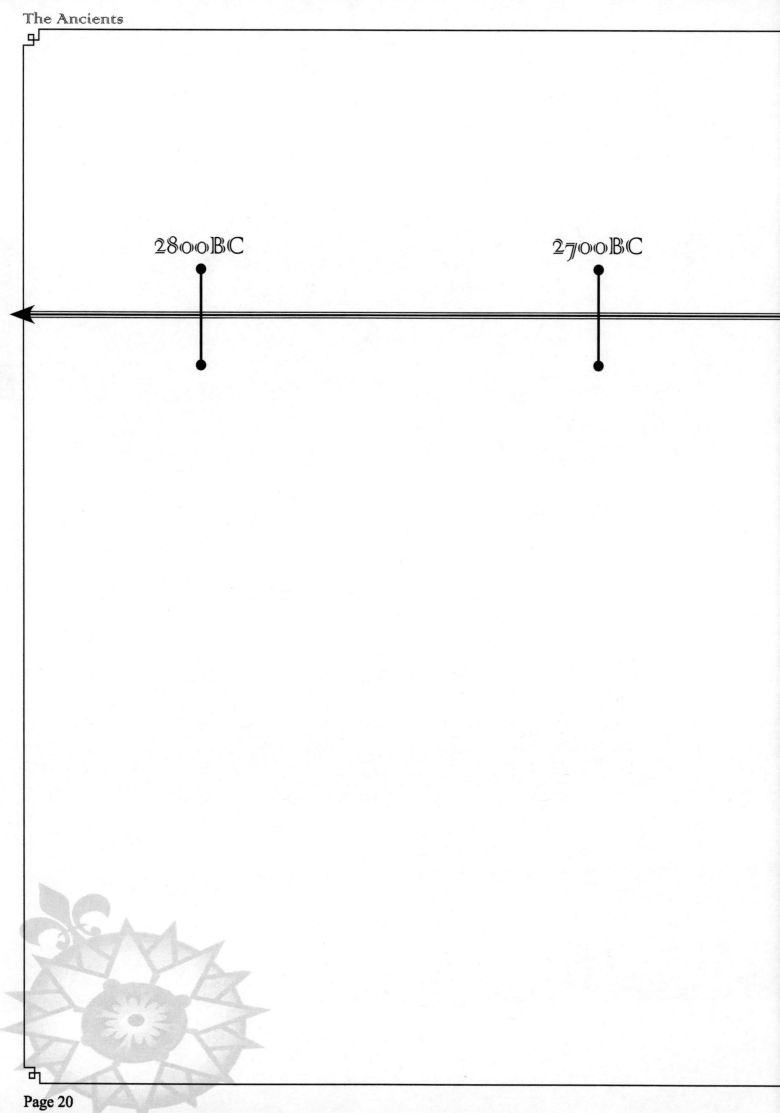

2800BC

2700BC

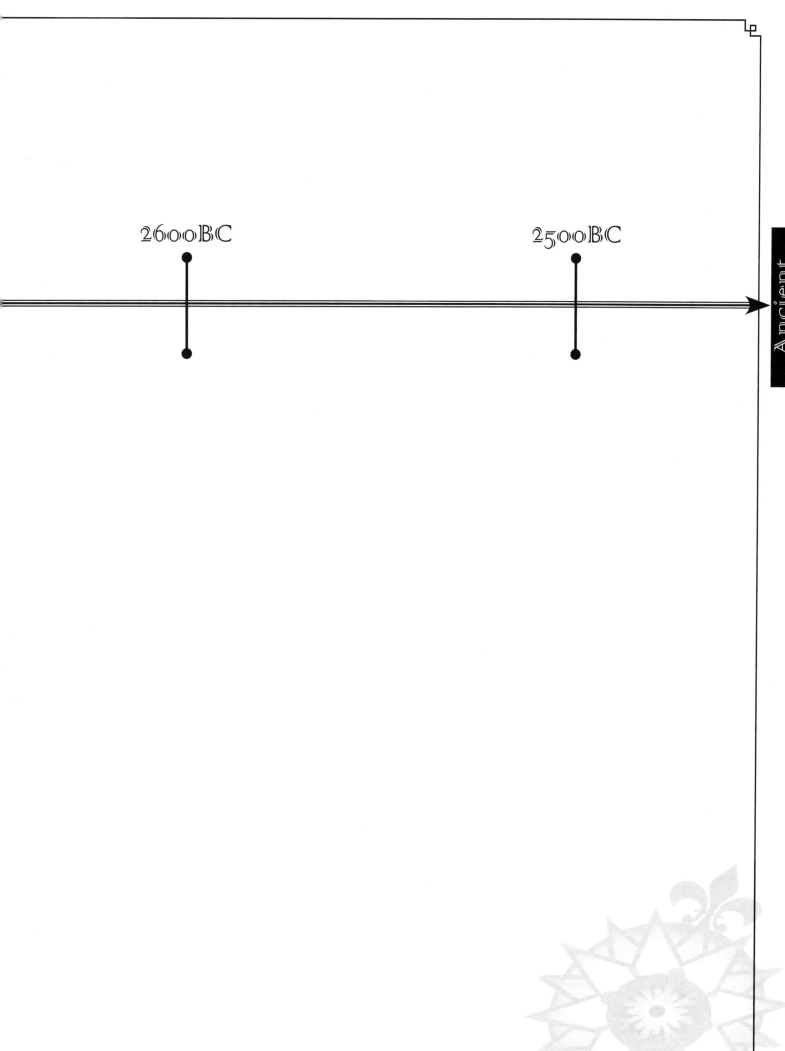

2600BC

2500BC

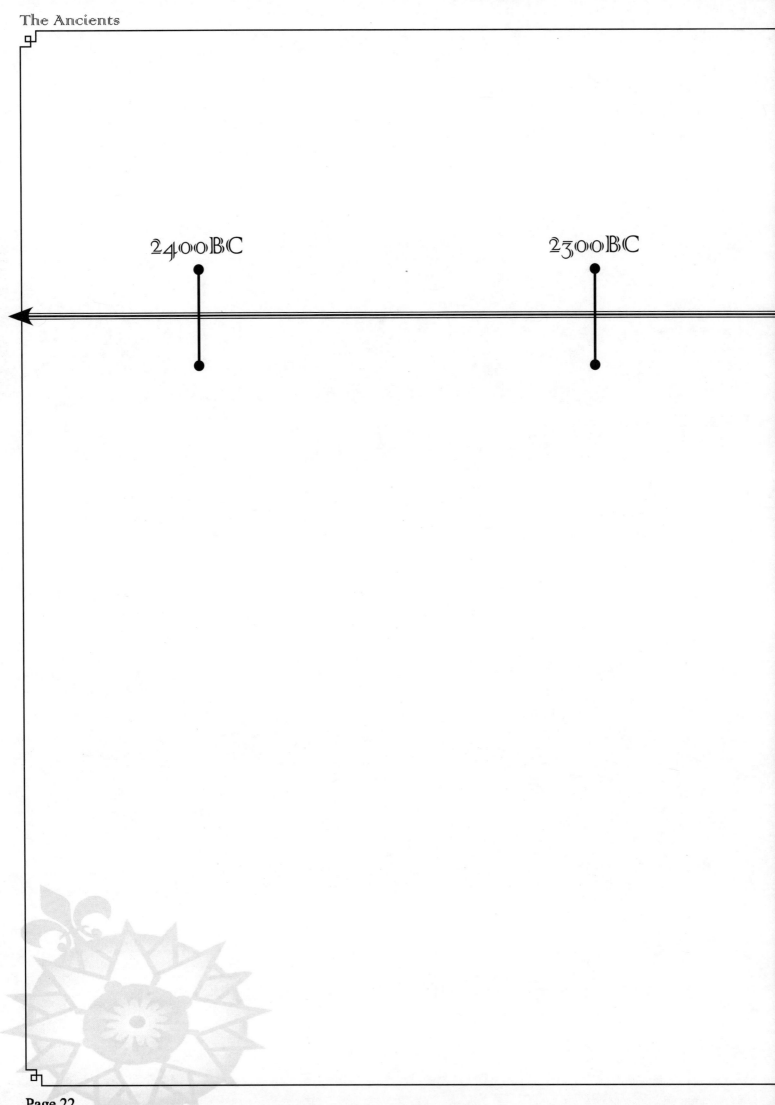

2400BC

2300BC

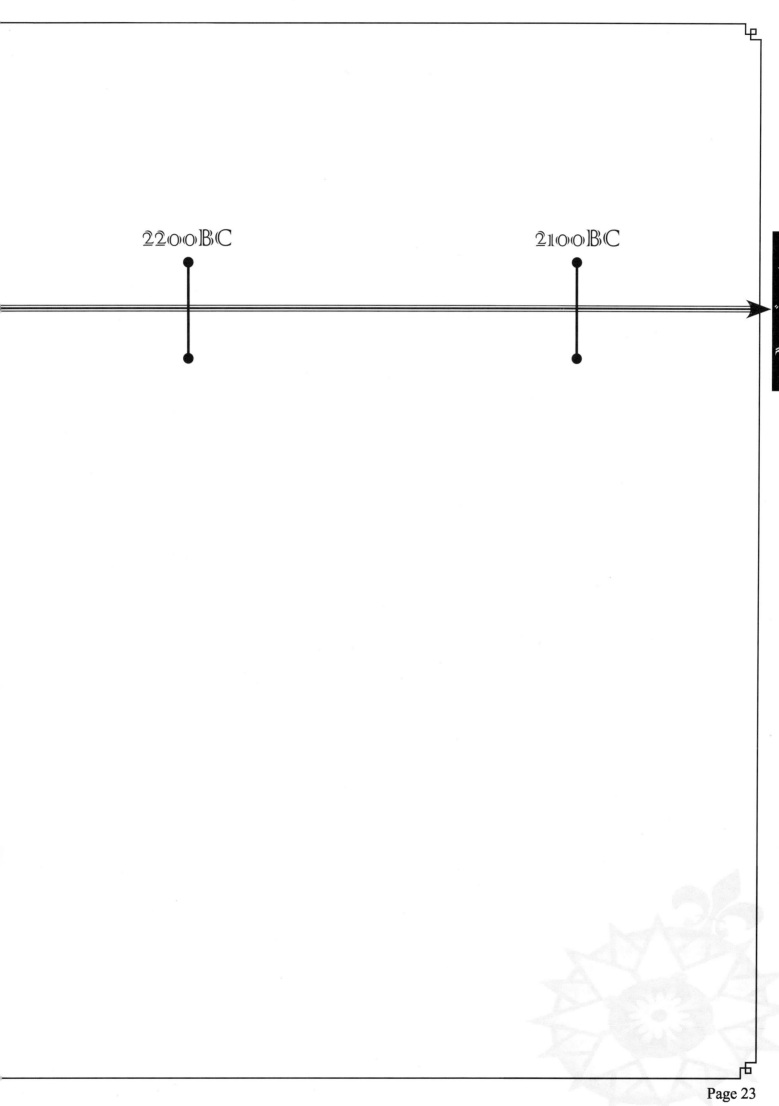

2200BC

2100BC

Ancient

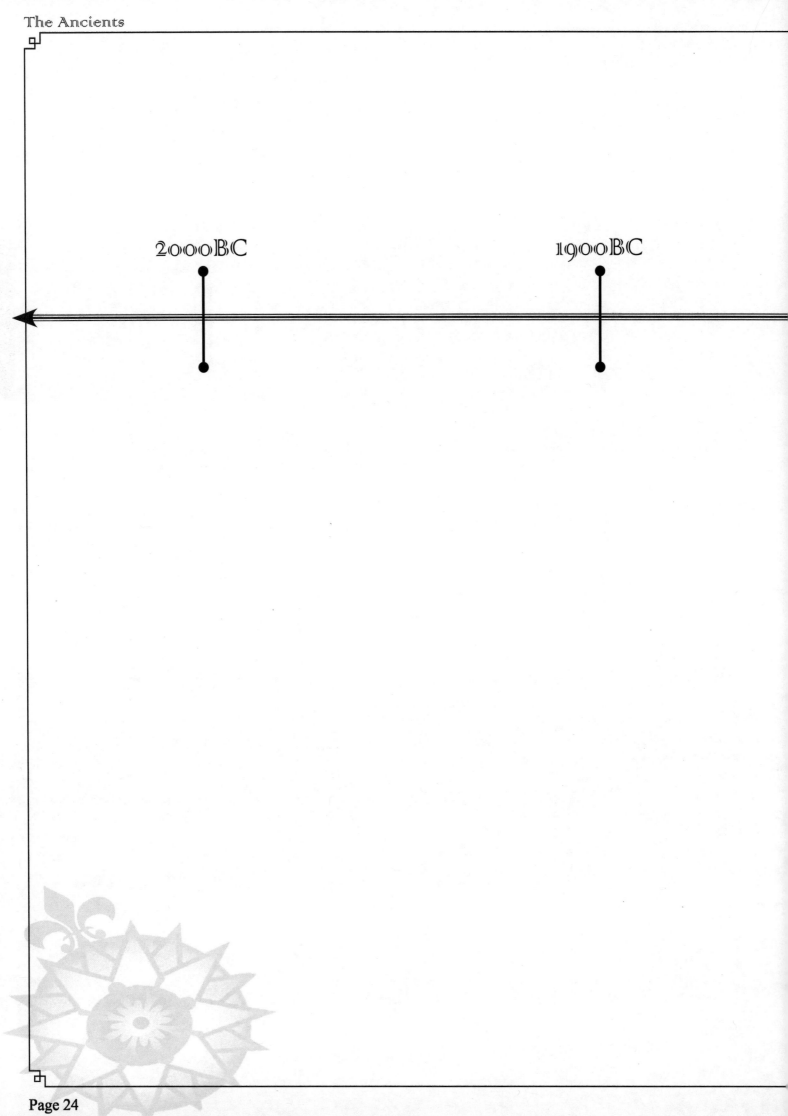

2000BC

1900BC

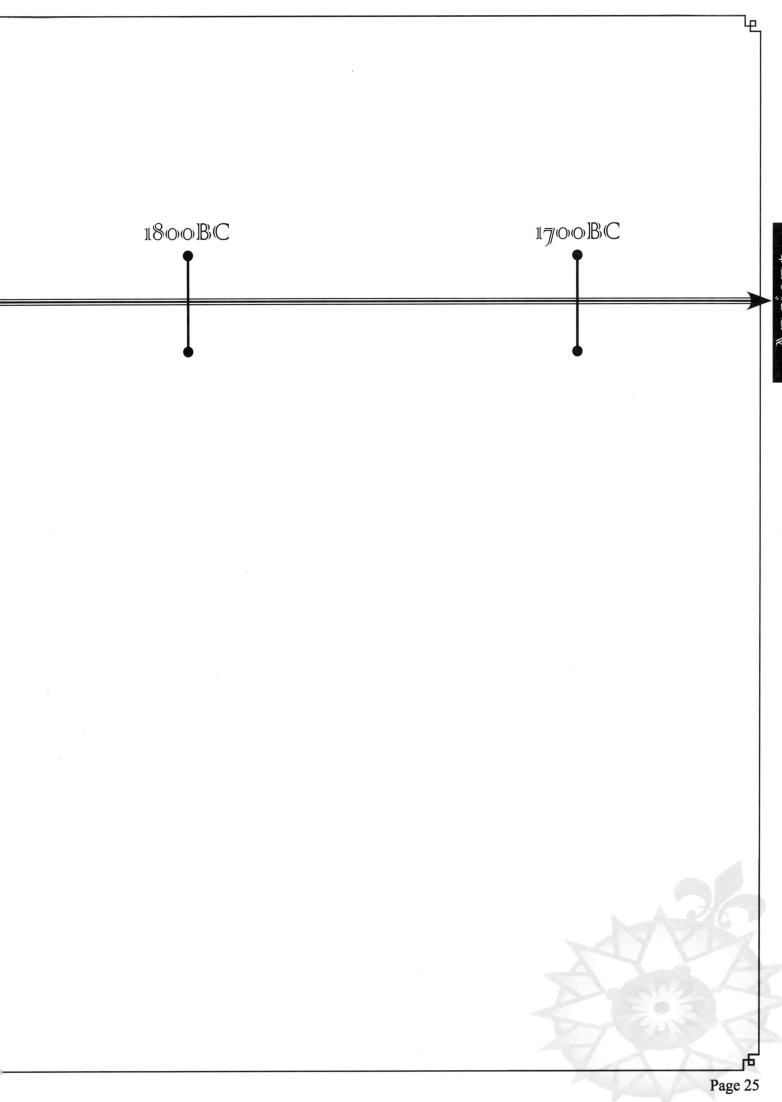

1800BC

1700BC

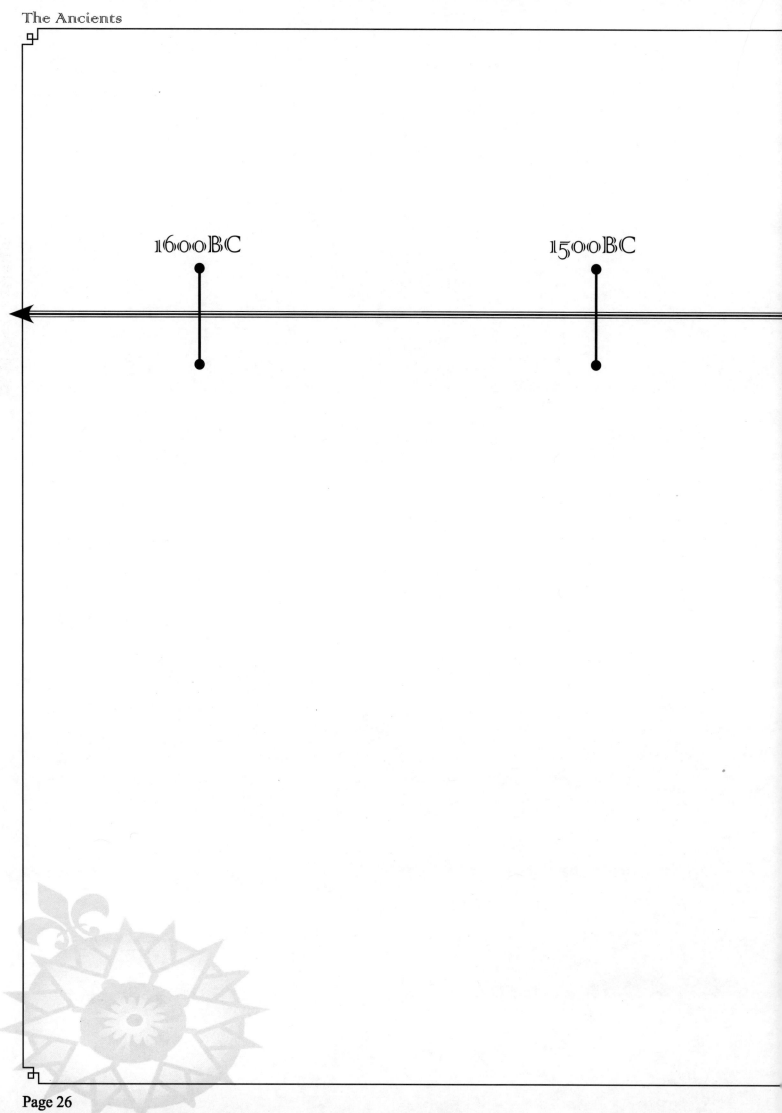

1600BC

1500BC

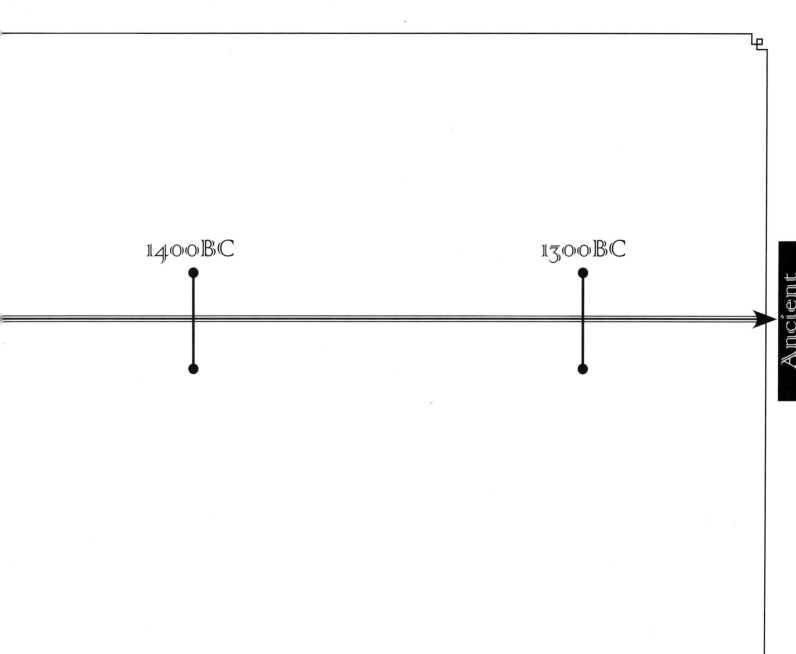

1400BC

1300BC

1200BC

1100BC

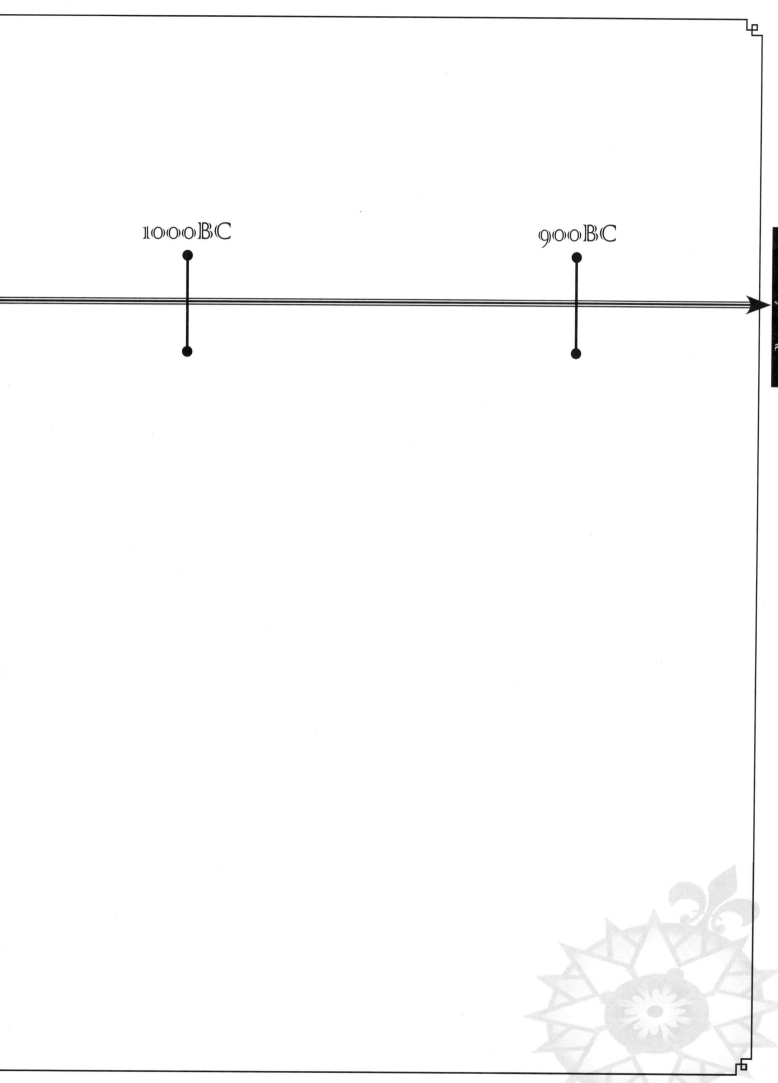

1000BC

900BC

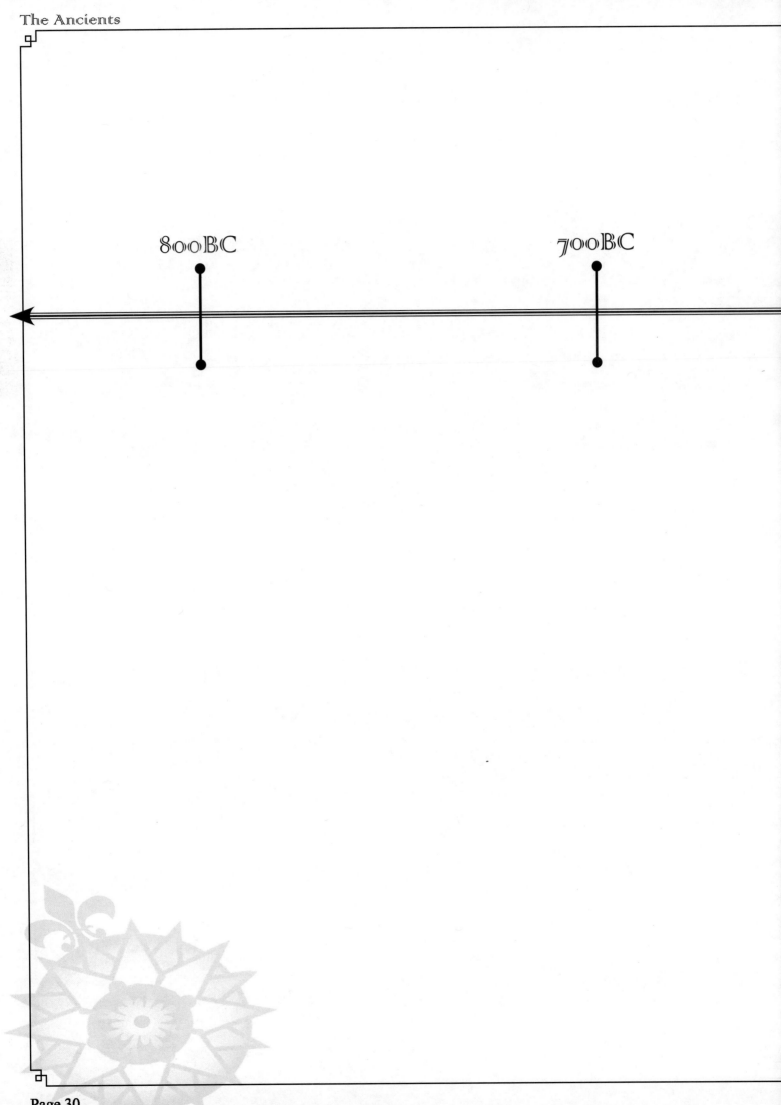

800BC

700BC

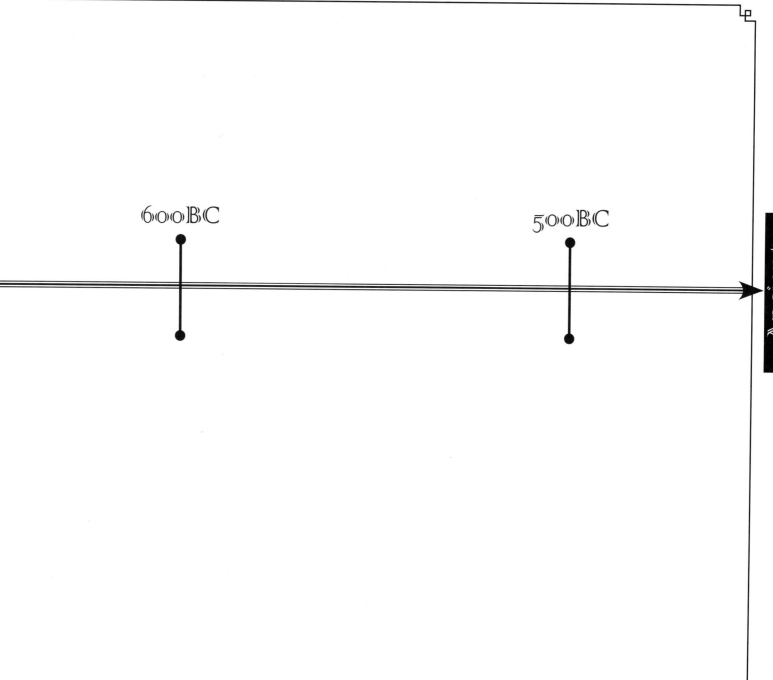

600BC

500BC

400BC

300BC

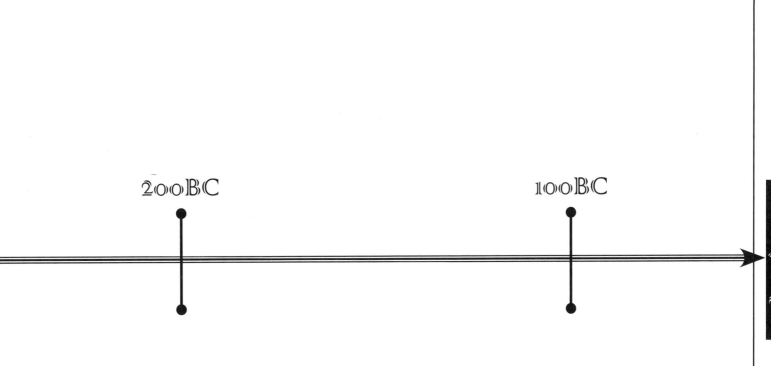

200BC

100BC

Ancient

1

100AD

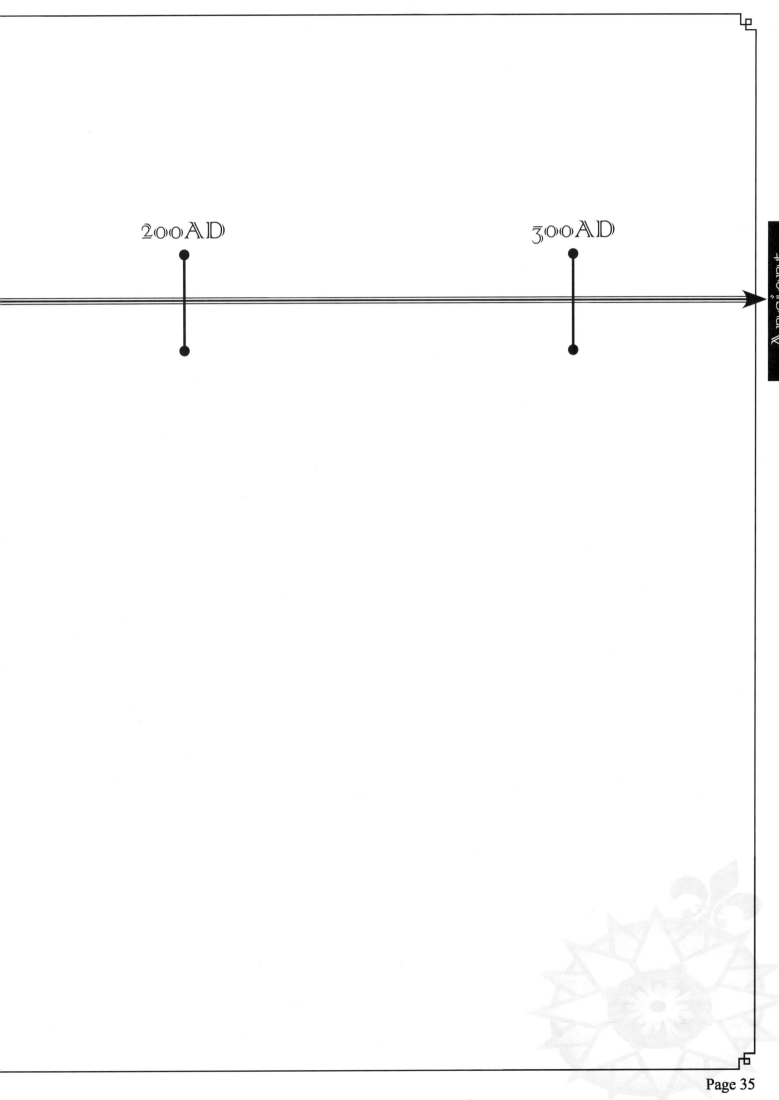

200AD

300AD

400AD

Significant Dates* to Consider for the Ancient Time Period:

5000*	BC	Farming begins in the fertile crescent
5000	BC	Farming begins in the Nile valley
5000	BC	Jericho grows into a wealthy town
5000	BC	Catal Huyuk is at its largest
4500	BC	First farmers in western Europe
4300	BC	First megaliths built in Brittany and Ireland
3900	BC	The Great Flood (date varies considerably among resources)
3500	BC	The wheel is invented
3500	BC	The Tower of Babel
3500	BC	Farmers settle in the Indus Valley
3300	BC	Growth of towns in Nile valley
3300	BC	Development of hieroglyphics
3100	BC	Menes unites Upper and Lower Egypt
3100	BC	Cuneiform writing is used
3000	BC	Building of Stonehenge has begun
3000	BC	First Chinese towns appear
3000	BC	Sahara desert dries up
2920	BC	The first pharaohs
2750	BC	Farming begins in West Africa
2700	BC	Huang Di becomes emperor of China
2600	BC	Ceremonial sites built in Peru
2575	BC	Old Kingdom of Egypt
2550	BC	The Great Pyramid is completed
2500	BC	Indus Valley civilization at its greatest (until 1800BC)
2500	BC	Towns begin to grow up in Crete
2500	BC	Royal tombs are built at Ur
2500	BC	Assyrians settle the upper Tigris valley
2200	BC	Period of Xia dynasty – Yu is the emperor
2200	BC	Mexican farming villages begin
2100	BC	The king of Ur rules Sumer and Akkad
2100	BC	The ziggurat at Ur is built
2040	BC	Middle Kingdom of Egypt
2000	BC	The Mycenaeans settle in Greece
2000	BC	The Hittites settle in Anatolia
2000	BC	The Amorites invade Akkadia
2000	BC	Peak of megalith building – Stonehenge nearly complete
1800	BC	Abraham settles in Canaan
1792	BC	Hammurabi rules Babylon (until 1750BC)
1766	BC	Shang dynasty begins rule in China
1720	BC	Egypt is invaded by the Hyksos
1700	BC	Crete at its most powerful (until 1450BC)
1680	BC	Assyria falls to the Hurrians
1595	BC	Hittites raid Babylon

1550	BC	New Kingdom of Egypt
1500	BC	The Aryans invade the Indus Valley
1450	BC	The Mycenaeans invade Crete
1400	BC	Phoenicians develop the first alphabet
1400	BC	Peak of Shang dynasty
1380	BC	King Shuppiluliuma rules the Hittites
1300	BC	Assyria regains power
1280	BC	Rameses II makes peace with the Hittites
1250	BC	Troy is destroyed
1200	BC	The Exodus of the Israelites from Egypt (perhaps as early as 1446BC)
1200	BC	Olmec towns built in Mexico
1195	BC	The Hittites are defeated by the Sea Peoples
1150	BC	The Philistines settle in southern Canaan
1122	BC	Zhou dynasty replaces the Shang
1100	BC	The Greek Dark Ages (until 800BC)
1076	BC	Assyria fall to the Aramaeans
1020	BC	Saul becomes King of Israel
1000	BC	David becomes King of Israel (until 965BC)
965	BC	Solomon reigns in Israel (until 928BC)
926	BC	Israel is divided in two
853	BC	Assyria takes control of Babylon
814	BC	Carthage is built
800	BC	The Etruscan civilization emerges
800	BC	First city-states founded in Greece
776	BC	The first Olympic Games
753	BC	The founding of Rome
730	BC	Assyria at its greatest
721	BC	Assyrians invade Israel, dispersing the Jews
700	BC	Nubian kingdom of Kush flourishes
668	BC	King Ashurbanipal rules Assyria (until 627BC)
626	BC	Babylonians revolt against the Assyrians
612	BC	Fall of Assyria to the Babylonians and Medes
612	BC	Nineveh sacked by the Babylonians and Medes
604	BC	Nebuchadnezzar becomes king of Babylon
600	BC	Nok culture in Nigeria begins to grow
600	BC	Earliest Mayan temples built
594	BC	Reform of the Athenian constitution
587	BC	Babylonians destroy Jerusalem and deport many Jews to Babylon
559	BC	Cyrus the Great creates the Persian Empire (until 530BC)
540	BC	Persians conquer Ionia (Greece)
539	BC	Babylon conquered by Cyrus the Great of Persia
521	BC	Darius expands Persian Empire to its greatest point
514	BC	The Scythians fight off an attack by the Persians
509	BC	The beginning of the Roman Republic
486	BC	Xerxes I rules Persia (until 465BC)
480	BC	Greeks halt Persian expansion at Salamis

447	BC	The Parthenon is built in Greece
431	BC	Peloponnesian Wars – Athens against Sparta
404	BC	Athens falls to Sparta
390	BC	Rome sacked by the Celts
371	BC	Sparta declines in power
350	BC	Decline of the Olmecs (Mexico)
350	BC	Earliest Mayan city-states appear
337	BC	Philip of Macedon invades Greece
332	BC	Alexander the Great conquers Egypt
331	BC	Fall of Persia to Alexander the Great
321	BC	Chandragupta Maurya establishes Mauryan Empire in India
315	BC	Qin becomes leading state in China
306	BC	Romans defeat Etruscans
300	BC	Rome expands to dominate Italy
300	BC	Tiahuanaco, Peru founded
264	BC	Punic Wars
230	BC	King Qin Zheng begins to unify China by force
221	BC	Qin dynasty unites China for the first time in one empire
214	BC	Construction of the Great Wall begins
212	BC	Chinese script standardized
202	BC	Founding of the Han dynasty in China
202	BC	The fall of Carthage
200	BC	The Polynesians migrate to Tahiti and the Marquesas
200	BC	First African city, Jenne-jeno, is established
200	BC	Teotihuacan founded in Mexico
196	BC	The Rosetta Stone
185	BC	The Mauryan Empire of India collapses
146	BC	Rome conquers Greece
103	BC	Revolt by slaves in Rome
91	BC	War between Rome and Italian cities
88	BC	Civil war in Rome
63	BC	Cleopatra (death by suicide in 30 BC)
58	BC	The Gallic Wars (until 53 BC)
50	BC	Rome conquers France
49	BC	Julius Caesar takes control of Rome
27	BC	Augustus becomes the first Emperor of Rome
3	BC	The birth of Jesus of Nazareth in Bethlehem

-1- Anno Domini – The Year of our Lord

30	AD	The crucifixion of Jesus Christ
30	AD	Egypt becomes part of the Roman Empire
45	AD	Paul's missions begin to Greece, Anatolia and Rome (until 58AD)
58	AD	Paul travels to Rome
64	AD	Persecution of Christians in Rome under Nero
65	AD	The Christian Gospels are being written

75	AD	The Kushan invasion of India
79	AD	The destruction of Pompeii
100	AD	Buddhism spreads from India
100	AD	Paper is invented
100	AD	The Gospels are completed
100	AD	The Roman empire reaches its greatest extent
165	AD	The plague sweeps through the Roman Empire
200	AD	The Roman empire's road system is completed
212	AD	Roman citizenship granted to all inhabitants of the empire
269	AD	St. Anthony establishes Christian monasticism in Egypt
313	AD	Emperor Constantine converts to Christianity
320	AD	Rule by Chandragupta I of India (founder of the Gupta Empire)
324	AD	Constantinople founded as the new capital of the Roman Empire
325	AD	The first Council of Nicaea
366	AD	The Japanese invade southern Korea
367	AD	Scots, Picts and Saxons attack Roman Britain
370	AD	Barbarians attack the Roman empire
380	AD	Rule by Chandragupta II of India (Gupta Empire at its peak)
391	AD	Christianity becomes the official religion of the Roman Empire
400	AD	Polynesian people migrate to the Hawaiian islands
406	AD	Roman withdrawal from Britain, Gaul and Iberia
410	AD	The Visigoths sack Rome – the fall of Rome
441	AD	The Huns defeat the Romans
451	AD	Huns devastate Gaul and northern Italy
470	AD	Decline of the Gupta Empire in India
476	AD	Fall of the last Roman emperor – Romulus Augustus

Please note: Most dates prior to 650BC are considered approximate

Timeline of Medieval History

400 - 1600

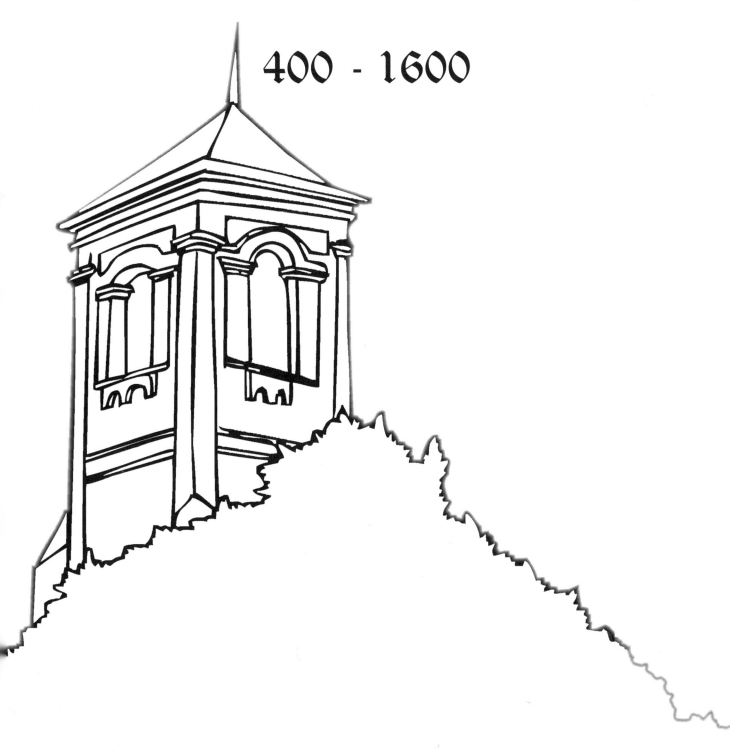

500

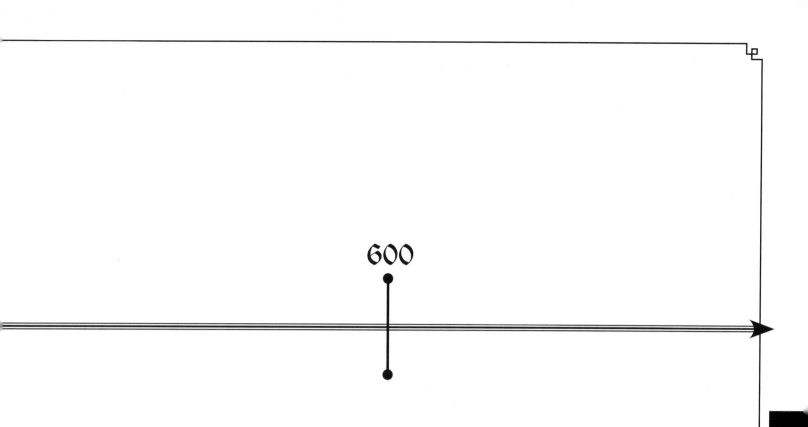

600

700

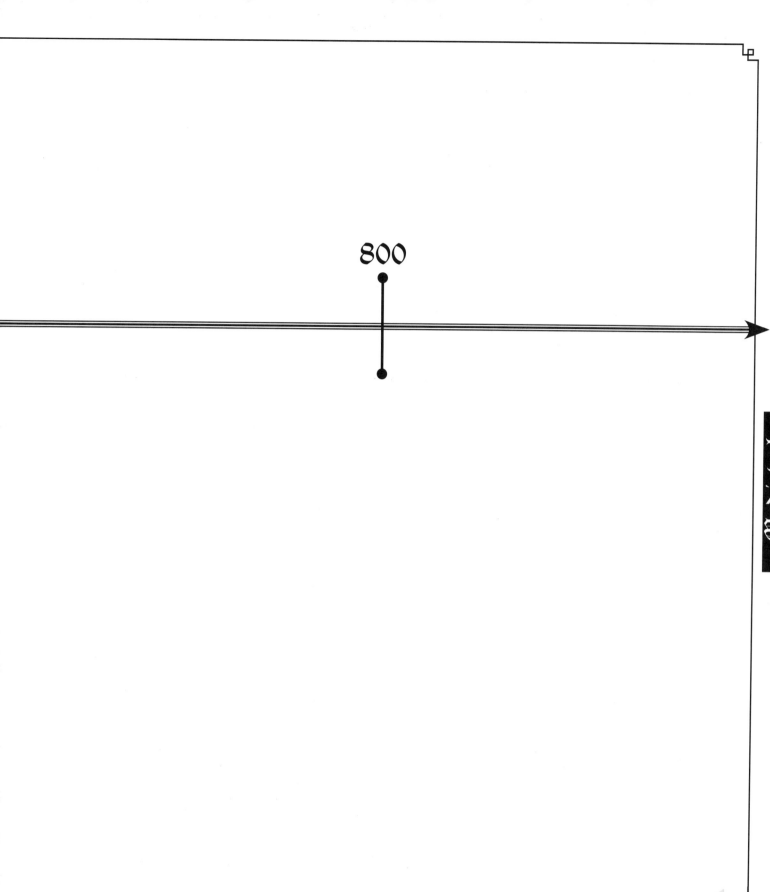

800

900

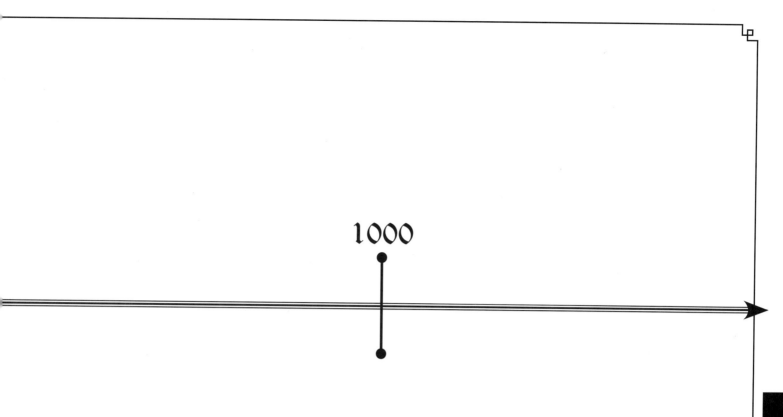

1000

1100

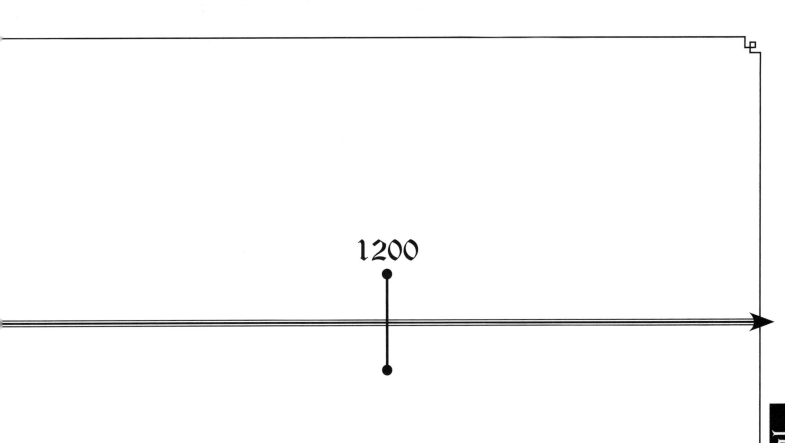

1200

1300

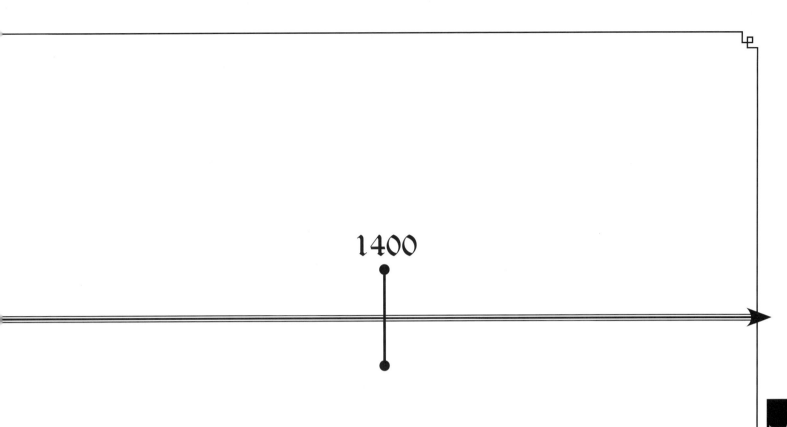

1400

1500

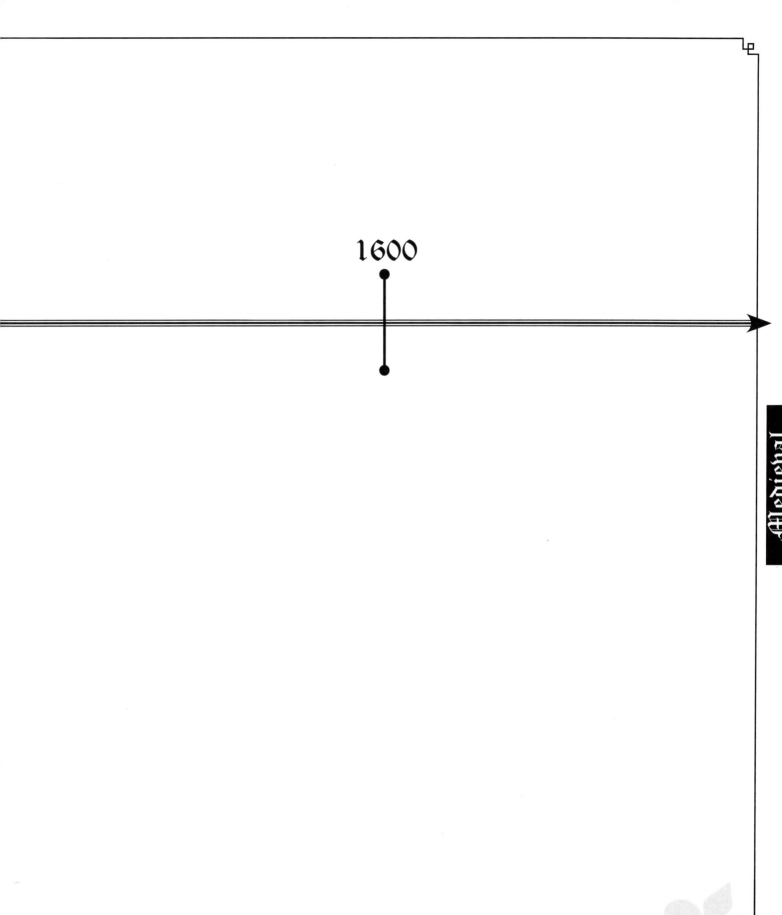

1600

Medieval

Significant Dates to Consider for the Medieval Time Period:

432	St. Patrick introduces Christianity to Ireland
476	The fall of the last Roman emperor
486	France united by Merovingian King, Clovis (until 510)
491	Anastasius, Emperor of the Byzantine empire (until 518)
527	Justinian and Theodora rule the Byzantine empire (until 565)
540	St. Benedict writes his Benedictine monastic rule
589	Yang Jian unites China, beginning Sui dynasty
597	Augustine arrives in Britain to convert the Saxons
600	Teotihuacan in Mexico is sacked and burned
610	Emperor Heraclius expands Byzantium
618	Tang dynasty founded by Li Jian
622	The flight from Mecca to Medina (the Hegira) takes place
630	Muhammad takes Mecca and forms an Islamic state
633	Arabs conquer Syria, Egypt and North Africa
636	Muslims capture Palestine, Syria, Persia and Egypt (until 642)
640	Chinese expansion in central Asia and Korea (until 660)
679	Bulgars conquer the Balkan territories
700	The epic of Beowulf
711	Arabs invade Spain
732	Franks defeat the Arabs at Poitiers, France
768	Charlemagne becomes Carolingian King
782	Charlemagne defeats the Saxons
790	Charlemagne defeats the Austrian Avars
793	The first Viking raid (Lindisfarne monastery)
794	Japanese court moves to a new capital at Heian on Kyoto
800	Pope crowns Charlemagne the emperor of the Holy Roman Empire
800	Toltec migration into Mexico
814	Charlemagne dies
843	Carolingian Empire divided into three (western Europe)
858	Fujiwara Yorifusa becomes regent of Japan
870	Danes immigrate into Danelaw
871	Alfred the Great becomes king of Wessex (until 899)
880	The Khmer conquer the Mon and Thai peoples in southeast Asia
896	Prince Arpad becomes leader of the Magyars (until 907)
900	Angkor Thom in Thailand is built
906	Moravia falls to the Magyars
907	Tang Dynasty collapses
920	Wenceslas tries to modernize Bohemia
955	Defeat of the Magyars, ending Magyar raids on Europe
960	Song Taizu founds the Song dynasty in China
976	Basil II rebuilds the Byzantine empire (until 1026)
983	The Vikings start a colony in Greenland
1000	Leif Ericson reaches North America

1013	The Danes conquer England
1054	Orthodox and Catholic churches split
1066	The Normans of France conquer England
1096	The First Crusade (until 1099)
1113	Angkor Wat in Thailand is built
1122	Eleanor of Aquitaine born
1127	The Jin conquer northern China and the Song retreat to Hangzhou
1133	Henry of Anjou born – death 1189
1137	Founding of Ethiopia by the Zagwe dynasty
1139	Eleanor of Aquitaine marries Louis VII of France; marriage annulled
1152	Henry marries Eleanor of Aquitaine
1154	Henry becomes king of England
1157	Birth of Richard I of England (the Lionheart) – death 1199
1166	Rory O'Connor becomes the first king of Ireland since 1014
1170	Murder of Thomas a Becket (becomes a saint in 1173)
1170	Norman invasion of Ireland
1180	Gempei civil war in Japan and the rise of the shoguns (until 1185)
1187	Saladin wins back Jerusalem
1189	Jewish massacre in York, England
1189	The Third Crusade (until 1192)
1200	Peak of the political power of the Roman Catholic Church
1200	Rise of the Aztecs and the Incas
1202	The Fourth Crusade ransacks Constantinople (until 1204)
1204	Norman Crusaders capture Constantinople
1209	Franciscan order receives papal approval
1212	The Children's Crusade
1215	Death of last Angkor king, Jayavarman VII (southeast Asia)
1215	King John signs the Magna Carta
1225	The Magna Carta becomes the law of England
1234	The Mongols conquer northern China and exile the Jin
1238	Invasion of Russia by the Mongols
1241	Collapse of Hungary after the Mongol raids
1248	The Christians reconquer most of Spain
1260	Peak of Bohemian power
1261	Byzantines retake Constantinople
1271	The travels of Marco Polo to China (until 1295)
1272	Edward I becomes king of England (until 1307)
1279	The Mongols conquer southern China and the Song dynasty ends
1290	Expulsion of Jews from England
1291	The last Crusades and Acre is defeated
1307	Edward II becomes king of England
1308	Bohemia and Moravia controlled by Germany
1337	The Hundred Years' War (until 1453)
1347	The Black Death sweeps through Europe (until 1351)
1353	The Black Death breaks out in China
1368	The Ming dynasty begins (until 1644)

1372	The birth of Jan Hus - death 1415
1378	The Great Schism (until 1417)
1381	The Peasant's Revolt is led by Wat Tyler (England)
1412	Birth of Joan of Arc
1419	The Hussite wars (until 1436)
1431	Joan of Arc burned at the stake (became a saint in 1920)
1438	Habsburg family controls the Holy Roman Empire (until 1806)
1440	Oba Eware the Great ruled Benin in West Africa (until 1473)
1452	Birth of Leonardo Da Vinci - death 1519
1453	Fall of Constantinople to the Ottoman Turks
1455	Johann Gutenberg prints the first book, the Bible
1462	Ivan III (the Great) strengthens Moscow (until 1505)
1469	The marriage of Ferdinand of Spain and Isabella
1477	The Netherlands become a Habsburg possession
1478	The Spanish Inquisition
1485	Henry Tudor comes to power in England (1457 – 1509)
1488	Dias rounds the Cape of Good Hope
1491	Birth of Henry VIII – death 1547
1492	The conquest of Granada
1492	Christopher Columbus discovers the West Indies (1451 – 1506)
1497	Vasco de Gama rounds the Cape of Good Hope
1499	Amerigo Vespucci discovers South America
1504	The Moguls seize Kabul in Afghanistan
1512	Michelangelo Buonarroti paints the ceiling of the Sistine Chapel
1516	Ferdinand of Spain dies (Isabella died in 1504)
1516	Charles V became king of Spain (1500 – 1558)
1517	Martin Luther nails a list of 95 theses to the church door at Wittenberg
1519	Ferdinand Magellan leads the first expedition to sail around the world
1522	Luther's Bible is published in German
1530	First Portuguese colony established in Brazil
1532	The Spanish invade the Inca Empire
1533	Ivan IV (the Terrible) expands Russia (until 1584)
1534	First African slaves are brought to Brazil
1534	England separates from the Roman Church
1540	John Calvin establishes the Protestant church in Geneva
1542	Mary Stuart becomes queen of Scotland when she is only 1 week old
1549	First Jesuit mission to Japan
1558	Elizabeth I becomes the queen of England and Scotland (1533 – 1603)
1562	The Huguenot Wars in France (until 1598)
1566	Calvinist church founded in the Netherlands
1572	The Massacre of St. Bartholomew's Day (France)
1580	Sir Francis Drake becomes the first Englishman to sail around the world
1581	The northern provinces of the Netherlands declare independence
1592	The Japanese invade Korea

Timeline *of* The New World

1600 - 1850

1600

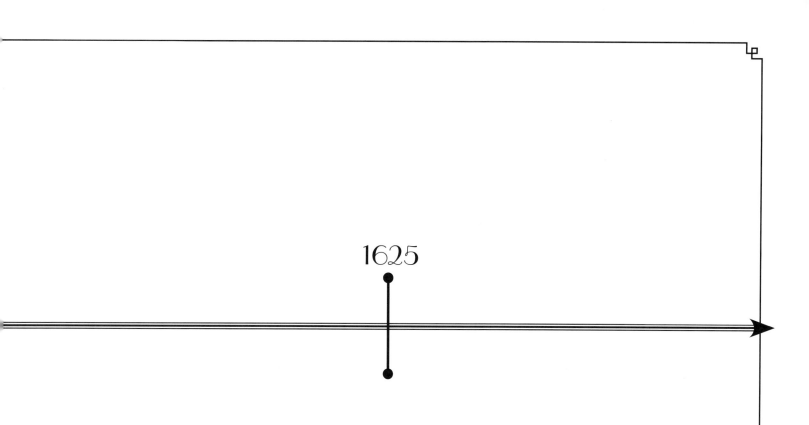

1625

1650

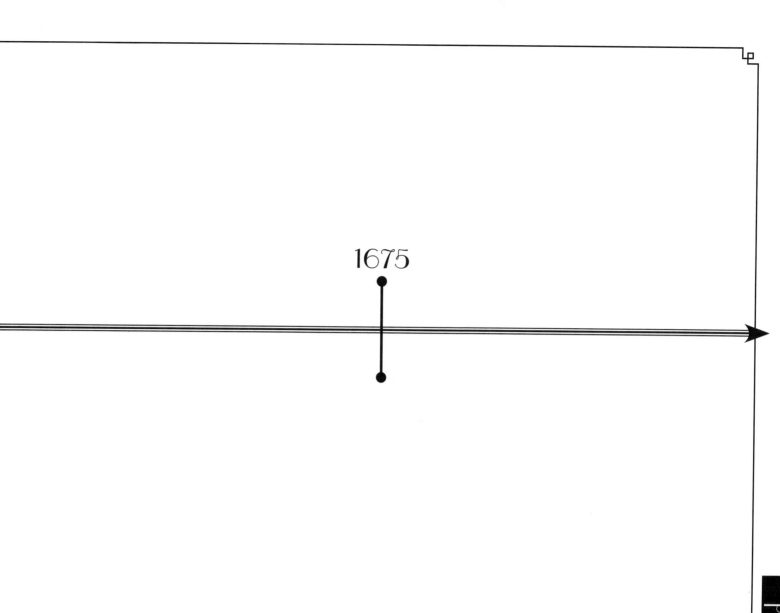

1675

1700

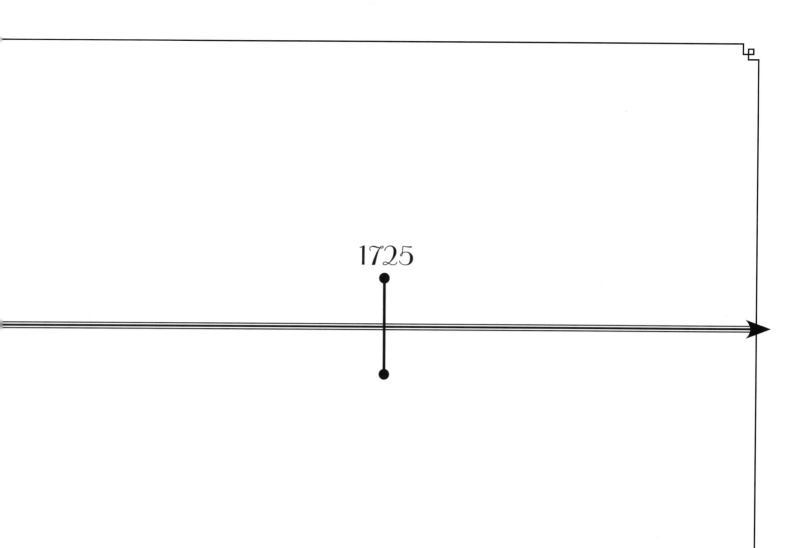

1725

1750

1775

1800

1825

Significant Dates to Consider for the New World Time Period:

1558	The reign of Elizabeth I (until 1603)
1564	The life of William Shakespeare – death 1616
1599	The Globe Theatre built in London
1600	The British East India Company is formed
1603	James I is king of England (until 1625)
1603	Samuel Champlain's arrives in Canada
1603	The Tokugawa shoguns rule Japan (until 1867)
1606	Dutch explorers reach Australia
1607	The English build a settlement in Jamestown, Virginia
1607	Henry Hudson voyages to the northeast
1608	Quebec colony established in Canada
1613	The Romanov dynasty of Russia begins
1618	The Thirty Years' War (until 1648)
1620	Arrival of the pilgrims in New England
1624	The Dutch settle in New Amsterdam (New York)
1625	Charles I is king of England
1630	Galileo Galilei proves that the Earth travels around the sun
1642	Abel Tasman reaches New Zealand
1643	Louis XIV is king of France (until 1715)
1644	The Manchu (Qing) dynasty rules in China (until 1912)
1648	The Republic of the United Netherlands is recognized by Spain
1648	Rebellion in Paris (until 1653)
1649	Parliament rules England (until 1653)
1660	Charles II is king of England (until 1685)
1660	Sir Isaac Newton discovers the laws of gravity
1661	Louis XIV regains control of France
1665	The Great Plague of London
1665	Charles II reigns as the last Spanish Habsburg king (until 1700)
1666	The Great Fire of London
1675	Christopher Wren begins to rebuild St. Paul's Cathedral
1680	The peak of the slave trade (until 1780)
1682	Peter the Great is tsar of Russia (until 1725)
1685	Johann Sebastian Bach - death 1750
1687	Sir Isaac Newton publishes *Principia Mathmatica*
1689	William of Orange is ruler of the Netherlands and king of England (until 1702)
1689	Russians swap Siberian land for trade in China
1690	John Locke publishes *Two Treatises of Government*
1692	The Salem Witch Trials
1695	Russia fights the Ottoman empire (until 1706)
1699	The French create the colony of Louisiana
1700	Russia fights Sweden (until 1721)
1701	The War of the Spanish Succession (until 1714)
1701	Frederick I is the first king of Prussia (until (1713)

1701	Jethro Tull invents seed drill for faster planting
1705	Edmund Halley predicts the return of Halley's comet in 1758
1707	The decline of the Moguls in India
1712	St. Petersburg becomes the new capital of Russia
1721	Johann Sebastian Bach composes the Brandenburg Concertos
1733	The British have 13 American colonies
1735	Carl Linnaeus classifies plants and animals
1737	The Persians invade northwest India
1737	The life of Thomas Paine – death 1809
1740	Maria Theresa rules the Habsburg empire (until 1780)
1740	Frederick the Great is king of Prussia
1750	China invades Tibet and Turkestan
1752	Benjamin Franklin discovers electricity
1754	The French and Indian War in North America
1756	The Seven Years' War (until 1763)
1757	Britain conquers major areas of India (until 1857)
1759	The British capture Quebec
1760	China invades Burma
1762	Catherine the Great is tsarina of Russia (until 1796)
1763	Treaty of Paris ends the Seven Years' War
1768	Captain Cook leads three sea voyages to the South Seas (until 1779)
1770	Ludwig von Beethoven - death 1827
1770	Cook claims Australia for Britain
1773	The Boston Tea Party
1775	The Battle of Bunker Hill (American Revolution)
1776	The 13 American colonies declare independence from Britain
1777	France joins the Americans in their war against Britain
1780	Wolfgang Amadeus Mozart plays for Empress Maria Theresa in Vienna
1781	British army surrenders at Yorktown
1782	James Watt invents a powerful steam engine
1787	The American Constitution is written
1789	George Washington becomes the first president of the United States
1789	The Bastille in Paris is overtaken by revolutionaries
1791	Thomas Paine writes *The Rights of Man*
1791	Bill of Rights is adopted
1791	Slaves revolt in Santo Domingo
1792	Denmark stops its slave trade
1793	Louis XVI and Marie Antoinette are executed
1793	The Reign of Terror in France (until 1794)
1794	Eli Whitney patents the cotton gin
1799	Napoleon takes control of France
1803	The Louisiana Purchase
1804	Slavery is made illegal in the northern United States
1805	Napoleon conquers most of western Europe (until 1812)
1805	The Battle of Trafalgar, October 21st
1805	Lewis and Clark reach the Pacific

1807	Robert Fulton's steamboat makes its first trip
1807	Abolition of slavery in England
1812	Napoleon invades Russia but is forced back
1812	The War of 1812 (until 1814)
1812	The birth of writer Charles Dickens - death 1870
1815	The Battle of Waterloo, June 18th
1815	Napoleon is imprisoned on the island of St. Helena until his death in 1821
1816	Simon Bolivar helps many South American states achieve their independence
1819	Spain gives Florida to the United States
1820	Britain claims the South African Cape Colony
1821	Mexico declares independence
1824	Mexico becomes a republic
1825	Bolivar creates the country of Bolivia
1827	Greece becomes an independent country
1830	All of the South American colonies are independent
1831	Nat Turner's Revolt
1833	Great Britain passes the Act of Emancipation
1835	The birth of Mark Twain (Samuel Clemens) - death 1910
1835	The Great Trek of the Boers
1836	The Battle of the Alamo
1839	The Opium War in China (until 1842)
1840	The birth of painter Claude Monet - death 1926
1840	The British take control of New Zealand
1841	David Livingstone begins to explore Africa
1843	Santa Ann becomes dictator of Mexico
1846	The Mexican-American War (until 1848)
1848	Gold is discovered in California

Timeline of the Modern World

1850 - the Present

1850

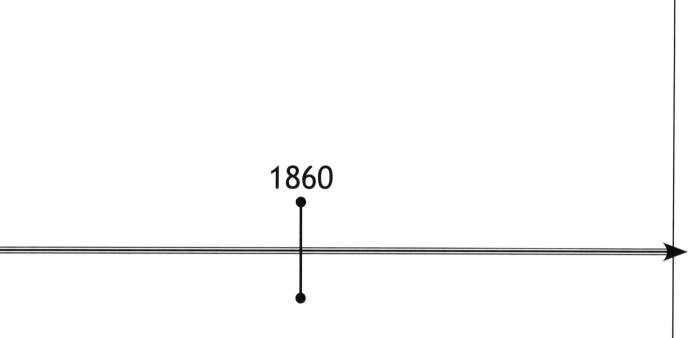

1860

1870

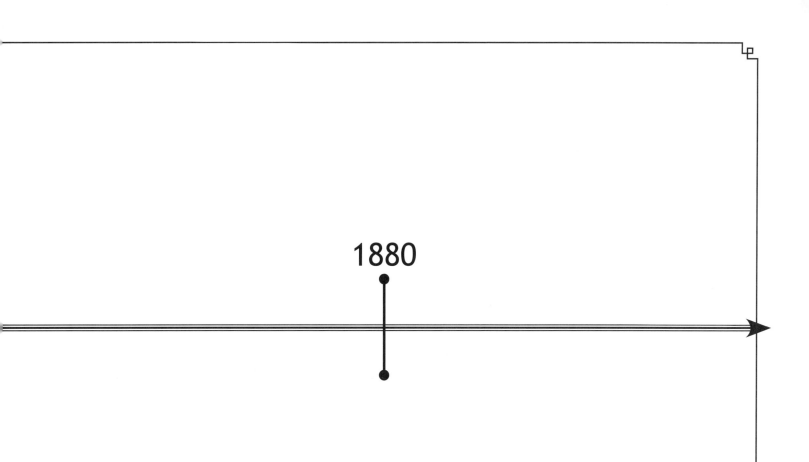

1880

Modern

1890

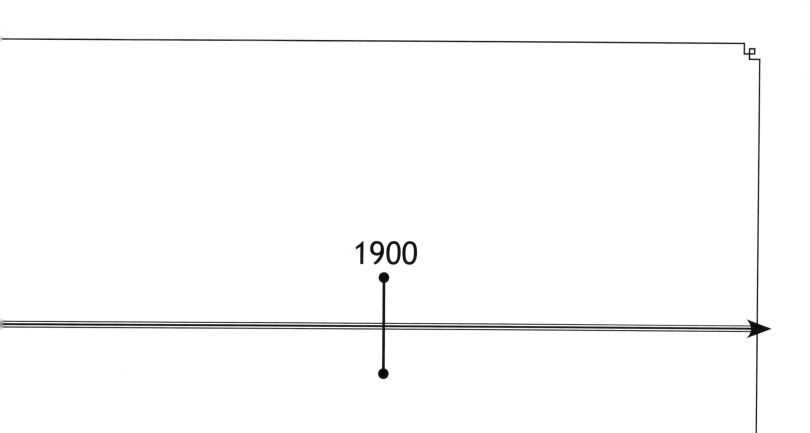

1900

Modern

1910

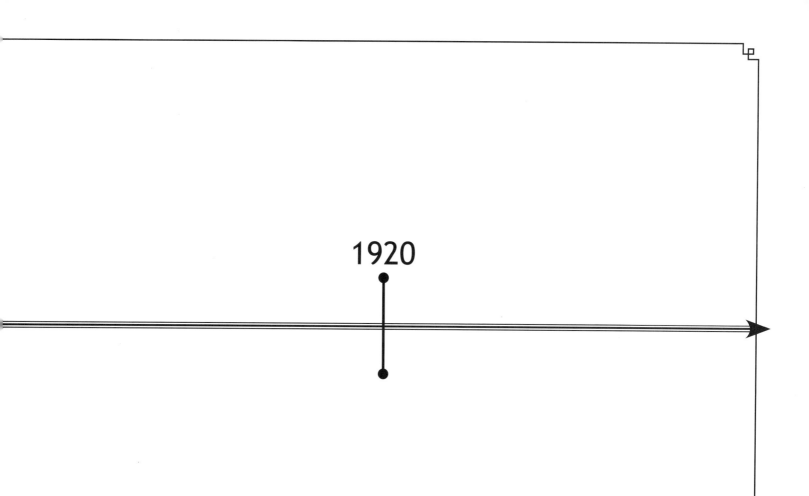

1920

Modern

1930

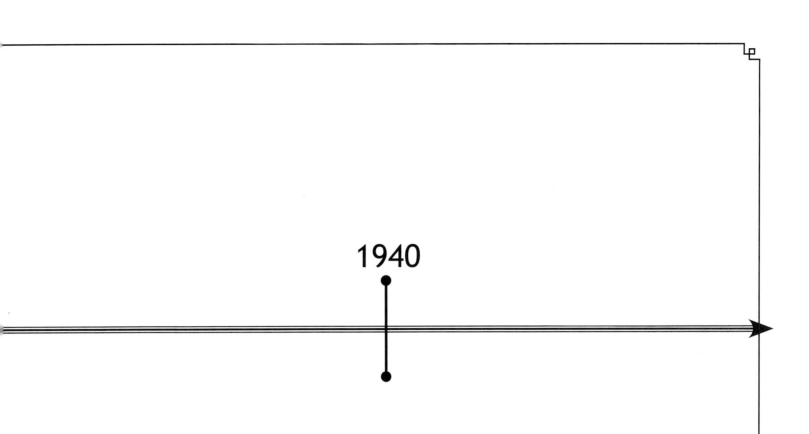

1940

Modern

1950

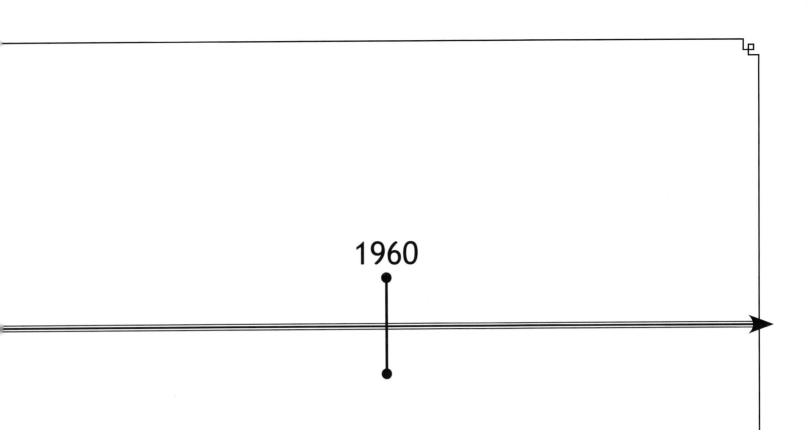

1960

Modern

1970

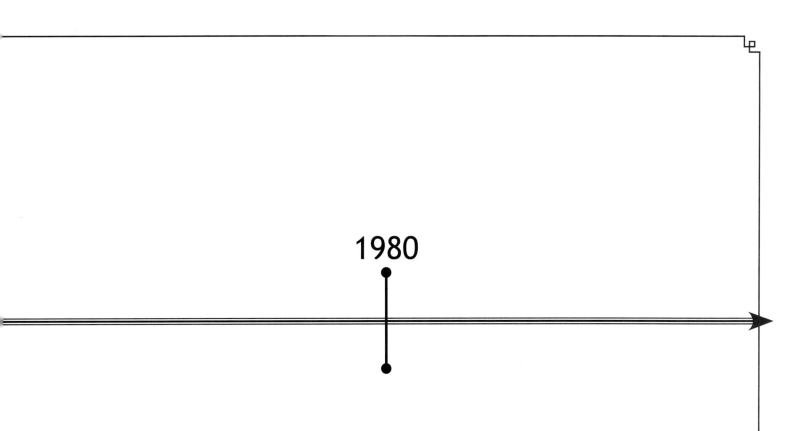

1980

1990

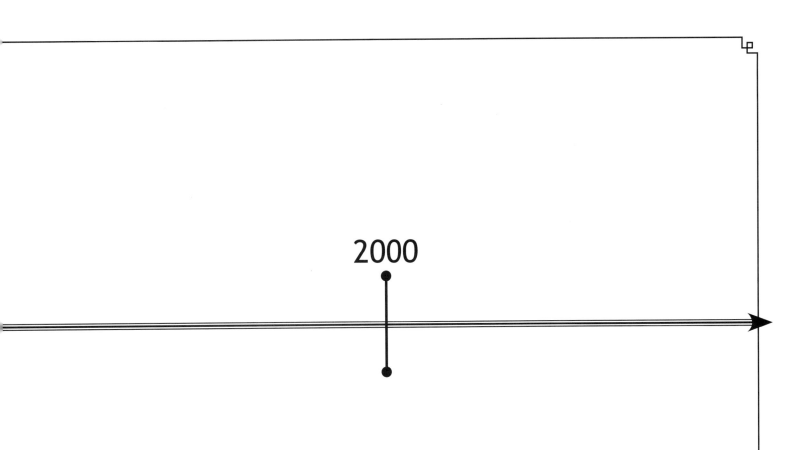

2000

2005

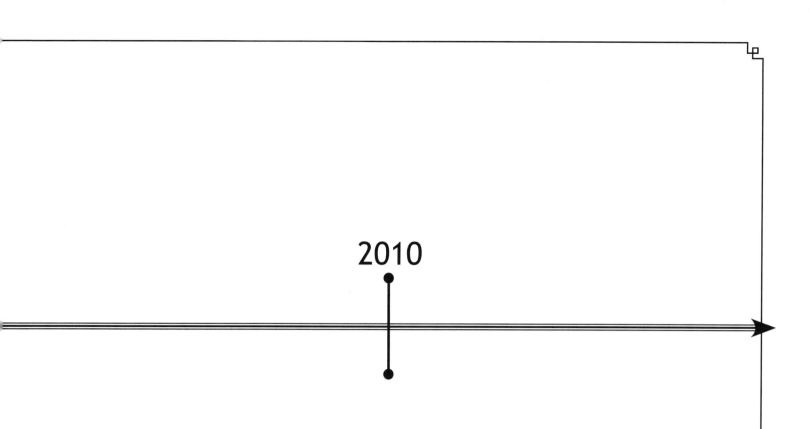

2010

Modern

Significant Dates to Consider for the Modern Time Period:

1845	Potato blight in Ireland causes widespread famine
1850	The Taiping Rebellion in China (until 1864)
1851	The Great Exhibition (Britain)
1851	Gold Rush starts in New South Wales (Australia)
1852	Napoleon III becomes emperor of France
1853	The Crimean War between Russia and Turkey (until 1856)
1854	Japan signs a trading agreement with the United States
1857	The Indian Mutiny (until 1858)
1857	The last Mogul Emperor gives up his throne
1858	The British government takes control of India
1860	Abraham Lincoln becomes President of the United States
1860	Native Americans fight the US army for their land (until 1890)
1861	The Italian states join together to form Italy
1861	Civil War breaks out in the United States
1863	The Battle of Gettysburg
1865	Slavery is make illegal throughout the United States
1865	The Civil War ends
1865	Abraham Lincoln is assassinated
1865	George Pullman invents the railroad sleeping car
1867	Nobel invents dynamite
1869	The birth of Mahatma Gandhi – death 1948
1869	The Suez Canal is completed
1869	Jules Verne writes *20,000 Leagues Under the Sea*
1871	Germany is united under Wilhelm I
1875	First telephone call made by Alexander Graham Bell
1876	The Battle of Little Bighorn (United States)
1879	Thomas Edison demonstrates the electric light bulb
1882	British occupy Egypt the protect the Suez Canal
1884	European leaders meet to divide Africa between them
1888	Slavery ends in the Americas
1888	George Eastman's Kodak box camera makes photography available to all
1889	The Eiffel Tower built in Paris
1890	The Native Americans are defeated at the Battle of Wounded Knee
1893	New Zealand becomes the first country to grant women the right to vote
1894	Japan fights China (until 1895)
1894	Nicholas II becomes tsar of Russia
1900	The Boxer Rebellion in China
1901	Commonwealth of Australia declared
1902	The British defeat the Boers
1903	Orville and Wilbur Wright make their first powered flight
1904	Japan fights Russia (until 1905)
1905	The Treaty of Portsmouth – Japan controls Korea
1907	New Zealand becomes a dominion within the British Empire

1908	Henry Ford produces Model T automobiles using an assembly line
1911	The Kuomintang starts a revolution in China
1912	The first Balkan War (2nd in 1913)
1914	Archduke Franz Ferdinand is murdered
1914	Austria-Hungary declares war on Serbia
1914	The Germans are defeated by the Allies at the Battle of the Marne
1917	The United States joins the First World War
1917	Riots break out in Petrograd and the tsar gives up his throne
1917	The Bolsheviks in Russia seize power
1918	The last Habsburg emperor gives up his throne
1918	The end of WWI
1918	Civil war in Russia (until 1921)
1918	Tsar Nicholas II and his family are shot by a group of Communists
1919	Benito Mussolini sets up the Fascist Party in Italy
1920	The Prohibition goes into effect in the United States (until 1933)
1920	The first radio stations are set up in the United States
1921	Vladimir Ilyich Ulyanov (better known as Lenin) controls Russia
1921	Albert Einstein wins the Nobel Prize for Physics (1879 – 1955)
1922	Russia is renamed the Union of Soviet Socialist Republics (USSR)
1922	Mussolini comes to power
1924	The death of Lenin
1928	Josef Stalin takes control of Russia
1929	The Wall Street stock market crashes
1929	The Great Depression (until 1939)
1932	Franklin D. Roosevelt becomes President
1933	Roosevelt launches the New Deal
1933	Adolf Hitler becomes chancellor of Germany
1934	Stalin's purges begin
1934	The Long March (until 1935)
1934	Hitler takes complete control of Germany as *Führer*
1937	Frank Whittle designs the first jet engine
1938	*Kristallnacht* – Nazis attack thousands of Jewish homes, shops and synagogues
1939	Britain and France declare war on Germany
1940	Hitler occupies most of western Europe
1940	The Battle of Britain
1941	Germany invades the Soviet Union
1941	Japan attacks US ships at Pearl Harbor, Hawaii
1944	The Allies land in France (D-Day)
1945	Adolf Hitler commits suicide
1945	Germany surrenders
1945	Hiroshima is destroyed by an atomic bomb
1945	The end of WWII
1945	The United Nations is formed to encourage world peace and protect rights
1947	India becomes independent
1948	Israel becomes a country
1949	Mao Zedong sets up the People's Republic of China

1949	NATO is formed – Germany is divided into East and West
1949	Apartheid is introduced in South Africa
1950	The Korean War (until 1953)
1953	Soviet Communist leader Josef Stalin dies
1954	The Vietnam War (until 1973)
1955	The Warsaw Pact is signed
1957	*Sputnik 1*, the first satellite, is launched
1958	Jack Kilby invents the first computer microchip
1961	The Berlin Wall is built
1961	Yuri Gagarin is the first person in space
1962	The Cuban Missile Crisis
1964	Palestinians form the Palestine Liberation Organization (PLO)
1964	Civil rights laws are passed in the United States
1965	Rhodesia becomes independent (renamed Zimbabwe in 1980)
1966	Mao Zedong starts the Cultural Revolution
1969	*Apollo 11* reaches the moon – Neil Armstrong walks on the moon
1971	E. Pakistan breaks away from W. Pakistan and is renamed Bangladesh
1971	The Soviets launch the world's first space station, *Salyut 1*
1975	The first small home computer is sold
1976	Mao Zedong dies
1979	Revolution in Iran
1979	The Soviet Union invades Afghanistan
1980	Most African states gain independence
1980	Iran – Iraq War (until 1988)
1981	The space shuttle makes its first flight
1981	The first PC is produced by IBM
1985	Mikhail Gorbachev becomes the leader of the Soviet Union
1986	The space shuttle *Challenger* explodes after lift-off
1989	East Germans cross the Berlin Wall
1989	Massacre in Tiananmen Square in Beijing, China
1989	British scientist Tim Berners-Lee creates the World Wide Web
1990	Hubble Telescope launched into space
1990	Iraq invades Kuwait
1990	East and West Germany become united
1990	Apartheid ends in South Africa
1991	The Gulf War
1991	The Cold War ends
1991	The Soviet Union becomes divided
1998	The first two parts of the International Space Station link up
2001	9-11 – hijacked planes crash deliberately into the World Trade Center

❧ My Notes ❧

❧ My Notes ❧

❧ My Notes ❧

❧ Ordering Information ❧

We hope that you have been pleased with your timeline book purchase. Knowledge Quest also has wall timelines available, as well as timeline figures, timeline software and historical blackline maps. Should you wish to order another copy of this book, or any of the above mentioned products, please visit us online at: www.knowledgequestmaps.com.

Write or call for your free catalog:

Knowledge Quest
Post Office Box 474
Boring, OR 97009-0474
Tel: 503.663.1210
Fax: 503.663.0670
inquiries@knowledgequestmaps.com
www.knowledgequestmaps.com

*Products and prices are as follows:

Wonders of Old: Timeline Book of World History	$21.95
Wonders of Old on CD-ROM	$21.95
Wall Timeline of Ancient History	$17.95
Wall Timeline of Medieval History	$17.95
Wall Timeline of New World History	$17.95
Wall Timeline of Modern History	$17.95
Timeline Category Symbols (stickers)	$7.95
HTTA Timeline Figures - Creation to Christ	$19.95
HTTA Timeline Figures - Resurrection to Revolution	$19.95
HTTA Timeline Figures - Napoleon to Now	$19.95
HTTA Timeline Figures - America's History	$29.95
Easy Timeline Creator on CD-ROM	$29.95
Blackline Maps of World History - The Ancients	$10.95
Blackline Maps of World History - The Middle Ages	$10.95
Blackline Maps of World History - The New World	$10.95
Blackline Maps of World History - The Modern World	$10.95
Unlabeled Maps of the US, World, and Selected Regions	$5.95
The Complete Set of Blackline Maps (binder)	$34.95
The Complete Set on CD-ROM	$29.95
Blackline Maps of American History	$24.95
Blackline Maps of American History on CD-ROM	$19.95
The Story of the World, Vol 1	$16.95
The Story of the World Activity Book 1	$29.95
The Story of the World Audiobook 1	$39.95
The Story of the World, Vol 2	$16.95
The Story of the World Activity Book 2	$29.95
The Story of the World, Vol 3	$16.95

* Prices subject to change